Péter Mujzer

History of 39/40 M. Csaba Armoured Cars in World War 2

KAGERO
publishing

inCOMBAT

39/40 M. Csaba armoured cars in World War 2 • Péter Mujzer

First edition • LUBLIN 2022

Acknowledgements

I would like to thank the following individuals and institutes for their kind support in terms of information and photographs, without which this book might not have been possible.

Photo credits **Bonhardt Attila, Deák Tamás, ECPA, Fortepan, Gőgh Gábor, Illésfalvi Péter, Karai Sándor, Markó Ferenc, Móker József, Mujzer Péter, Pálinkás Zsolt, Tóth Marcel, Sárhidai Gyula, Szollár János, Virág Ajtony, War Correspondent Company.**

Colour profiles: **Arkadiusz Wróbel**

Drawings: **Bajtos Iván, Benczúr László, Service manuals**

Tactical maps based on original maps published in the Hungarian Military Review from 1942 to 1944

DTP: **KAGERO STUDIO**

ISBN: 978-83-66673-99-1

Printed in Poland

KAGERO Publishing • e-mail: kagero@kagero.pl, marketing@kagero.pl
Editorial office, Marketing, Distribution: KAGERO Publishing,
Akacjowa 100, os. Borek – Turka, 20-258 Lublin 62, Poland, phone/fax +48 81 501 21 05

www.kagero.pl • shop.kagero.pl

Table of Contents

INTRODUCTION

The armoured cars were light-weighted wheeled armoured fighting vehicles, employed for reconnaissance, internal security, armed escort and subordinate battlefield tasks during WW2. With the gradual decline of the cavalry, armoured cars were developed for carrying out duties formerly assigned to light cavalry. Following the invention of the tracked armoured vehicles, the armoured cars remained popular due to their faster speed, comparatively simplified maintenance and low production costs.

During WW2, the belligerent armed forces used light, medium and heavy armoured cars. The light armoured or scout cars were two-axes, four-wheeled all-terrain lightly armed and armoured vehicles, with a crew of 2-3. The medium armoured cars were larger, better armoured with cannons and machine guns, while the heavy armoured cars with three-four-axes could carry a wide range of weapons up to heavy anti-tank guns.

At the beginning of WW2, even the major forces had a mixture of late 20s early 30s designs as well as brand new armoured cars in their possession. The surrounding East-European countries also employed indigenous and export armoured cars. The Polish Army had the late 20s designes; wz.29 and 34 armoured cars. The Czechoslovakian Army had the home-produced Skoda PA II light, Tatra OA vz.27and 30 medium armoured cars. The Austrian Army had the Daimler ADGZ heavy and ADKZ light armoured cars. The Romanian Army only had 13 ex-Czechoslovakian Tatra and Skoda armoured cars in 1941.

The Treaty of Trianon prohibited any kind of armoured vehicle or armoured troops for the Hungarian Army. However, the leadership of the Army recognised the importance of this new branch and equipment and remembered the successes that had been achieved by the use of armoured trains and armoured cars during WWI.

By the end of the 1930s, the Hungarian Army was able to put together the theoretical, organisational requirements with the financial and industrial background to have its armoured cars following the developments of the Armoured Troops 1938-1939.

The Hungarian 39 M. Csaba armoured cars were designed and developed in cooperation of the Hungarian born, then English citizen Nicholas Straussler, the engineers of the Weiss Manfred Company and the Military Technology Institute of the Hungary Army (HTI).

Based on the vehicles' classification the 39 M. Csaba armoured car was a well-armed light armoured car at the beginning of WW2. Later the weak firepower and armour protection, as well as the limited off-road capability significantly reduced its usability. Against all odds, its characteristic form has become one of the symbols of the Hungarian armoured forces in WW2.

The pointed-nosed, relatively tall-built hull and the large turret with a slight slope suggested some English and French kinship. The 39 M. Csaba was regarded as comparable to the German Sd.Kfz.221 and 222, and the British Guy and Humber armoured cars too.

Naming the Hungarian produced armoured vehicles was always connected to the glorious past of Hungary. The Zrínyi assault howitzer was named after a famous Hungarian warlord fighting the Ottomans in the XVI Century. The Toldi light tank was named after a Hungarian warrior, Miklós Toldi who distinguished himself in the XIV Century. Csaba was a fictional Hungarian character, according to the legends one of the sons of Attila. Between the two sons of Attila was a struggle of inheritance, which cost the life of Csaba. But when his former supporters were in grave danger, according to the legend, Csaba returned from the Galaxy with his arching horsemen and saved his people.

The only Hungarian-built, armoured, wheeled vehicle of the Second World War was the 39/40 M. Csaba armoured car.

Standby armoured cars of the RUISK, prepared to counter internal disturbances in the late 20s, equipped with 29 M. Vickers and Rába V.P. armoured cars armed with 07 M. Schwarzlose machine guns. (Szollár János)

The combat vehicles were manufactured in series by Weiss Manfréd Factory in Csepel/Budapest.

The Csaba armoured cars were also the only wheeled armoured vehicles deployed by the Hungarians during WW2. According to common knowledge, no Csaba armoured car survived the war, although one 39 M. Csaba armoured car was exhibited by the Red Army at the War Booty Exhibition held in Moscow alongside the River Neva in the summer of 1945. But unfortunately, we have no information about the existing Csaba armoured car in the collection of the Tank Museum of Kubinka.

Two unarmed 29 M. Vickers armoured cars, belonged to the RUISK, painted dark blue, during a summer exercise in the early 30s. (Tóth Marcell)

Dummy armoured car built on a Fiat car, resembles the Czechoslovakian PA-II armoured car, armed with 07 M. Schwarzlose machine gun. (Deák Tamás)

The Hungarian Minister of Defence, General Vilmos Rőder and Austrian officers inspecting the Austrian made ADKZ heavy armoured car in 1937. (Mujzer collection)

Polish wz. 34 armored car in 1939, the wz. 34 was an outdated late 20s design used by the Polish armored reconnaissance troops during the Blitzkrieg. (Fortepan)

NICHOLAS STRAUSSLER AND HIS DESIGNS

Born in Hungary, Nicholas Straussler (1891- 1966) was an engineer, inventor and businessman who lived and studied in England during the interwar period. He was most famous for developing the flotation system used by the Allied amphibious DD tanks during the landing in Normandy in 1944.

Straussler travelled often between England and Hungary during 1928-33 and became a British citizen in 1933. In 1932 he developed the A.C.1, the experimental armoured car for the British Air Ministry, and in 1933 established Straussler Mechanisation Ltd for designing and building his vehicles and inventions. He came to Hungary in 1933 and agreed with the Weiss Manfréd Factory in Csepel to make prototypes of the vehicles he designed. The main reason for this was that Straussler Mechanisation Ltd's was lack of money to produce even a single prototype. The Automobile and Tractor Department of Weiss Manfréd Factory was comparatively cheap and had full design capacity. The A.C.1 armoured car prototype was made by Weiss Manfred in Csepel, Hungary, and then delivered to England.

A.C.1 ARMOURED CAR

The British Army ordered an off-road armoured vehicle from Straussler. The 70-horsepower engine of the tubular, two-axle, all-wheel drive and steering vehicle was placed above the rear axle. The three-point suspension of the swinging axles made it easier to travel in the field.

Nicholas Straussler was a Hungarian born engineer and businessman. (Mujzer collection)

The all-wheel-drive could be switched off. When switching from off-road to on-road, the vehicle was able to travel as a conventional car, with rear-wheel drive and front-wheel steering - reducing fuel consumption and making driving significantly easier.

The experimental A.C.1 armoured car was built in 1934 at the Weiss Manfred Factory, after a successful factory test, with a temporary hull made of wood panels; it made its way

The prototype of the A.C.2 armoured car, built by the Weiss Manfred Factory in 1935 with a temporary body, next to the A.C.2 is a Fiat Ballila car. (Fortepan/Korbuly)

Side view of the A.C.2 armoured car with a two-seater Fiat Ballila car, the A.C.2 superstructure was built of wooden plates instead of armour ones. (Fortepan/Korbuly)

The undercarriage and the leaf springs of the A.C.2 armoured car during the test drive in Hungary 1935. (Fortepan/Korbuly)

Chassis of the A.C.2 armoured car with 100 h/p engine with radial ventilator, with front and rear driver positions. (Fortepan/ Korbuly)

Chassis of the light artillery tractor designed for the British Army, this prototype was also built for Straussler at Weiss Manfred Factory in 1935. (Fortepan/ Korbuly)

The MT light artillery tractor had a 35 h/p engine and its speed was 30 km/h, the prototype was sent to England to Alvis Company in 1937. (Fortepan/Korbuly)

Straussler A.C.2 armoured car with 8mm armoured hull and turret built by Alvis Company, armed with Vickers machine gun. (Alvis Ltd.)

Straussler A.C.3D armoured car of the Dutch East-Indian Army with a redesigned armoured hull made of vertical armoured plates, armed with two Vickers machine guns. (Alvis Ltd.)

to England on its wheels. The trip lasted four days; the A.C.1 was driven alternately by Captain Emánuel Czaykowski from the Hungarian Military Technical Istitute (HTI) and mechanical engineer János Korbuly, then the chief engineer of the Weiss Manfred Factory, without any escort car or support. The field tests in Aldershot has contributed to the development of a more advanced version of the design. The work at the Weiss Manfred Factory was also monitored by experts of the HTI. The Hungarian military leadership positively acknowledged the A.C.1 armoured car chassis for its excellent off-road capabilities, however, the Hungarian Army was still forced to relinquish the use of the patent - mainly for financial reasons - at that time.

Nicolas Straussler remained the owner of A.C.1 in Aldershot, and in 1934, summarizing his experience, ordered the prototype of the A.C.2 armoured car as well. From Straussler, the RAF ordered a reconnaissance armoured vehicle for desert use, which was the A.C.2. The engine was Weiss Manfred's property, a V-8 100-hp engine. It was a unique type, but suitable for experimental purposes. The inflow of cooling air was made independent of the direction of travel. This made it possible to lock the rear armour of the vehicle, which improved the protection.

The A.C.2 armoured car also had the "rear" driver's position, which was already a requirement for armoured vehicles for reconnaissance purposes. The "rear" driver's compartment was also equipped with all the instruments needed to drive the vehicle. Due to the all-wheel drive, driving the vehicle in the field required a great deal of force. This was facilitated by the installation of a two-speed steering gear, which in turn further complicated the otherwise simple mechanism.

Two A.C.2 armoured cars were made at the Weiss Manfred Factory in Csepel. One left for England in the spring of 1935 with a temporary superstructure accompanied by a WM Factory's escort car.

The road led through Zurich and Bern and was presented at the Military Academy in Nauheim, Germany. The British Army tested and ordered the final cassis of the armoured car. This was made in Coventry by the Alvis Factory, made of an 8mm armour plate, following the outline of the wooden hull designed in Csepel. A water-cooled Vickers machine gun was placed in the turret. The armoured car was tested in 1935 in Iraq. Based on its modern design and good off-road capability, it also performed well in desert conditions. The positive experience with the A.C.2 armoured car led the British Department of Defence and the Air Force Command to order a smaller series of combat vehicles. Fifty chassis were produced - according to the Company records in England; these were made in the same design as the A.C.2 armoured car at the Weiss Manfréd Factory in Hungary. The A.C.2 superstructure was made of by the Alvis Factory in England. Later, it was produced with a 120-hp, Alvis series engine. In addition to the machine gun in the turret, its armament was reinforced with another machine gun placed next to the driver.

A.C.3D ARMOURED CAR

From this version, 12 went to the Dutch East India Army and three to the Portugal Army. Another 12 were bought by the British Air Force, on which minor changes were made. To increase the size of the fighting compartment, vertical side plates were used. The machine gun next to the driver was replaced by a double driver's window. Despite successful testing, the Alvis-Straussler combat vehicle marked Type "A" was eventually not put in service, so production of the A.C. armoured car series in England ceased in 1938. At that time, Straussler's relationship with the Alvis Factory was severed, and no more armoured car designs were made. There were three prototypes, the use of 23 other vehicles could not be determined; the superstructure was probably completed for them, but no further information was available about their fate.

The Portugal connection had an interesting follow-up story, the Portugal Ministry of Defence examined the possibility of purchasing 39 M. Csaba armoured cars from the Weiss Manfred Factory around 1940, but due to the coming war and the limited capacity of the Factory it did not materialise.

Two A.C.2 armoured cars were built in Csepel, already with the support of the Hungarian Ministry of Defence. One left for Britain, the other remained in the factory. The modern construction, which was not a semi-solution, made of a truck chassis, but a vehicle originally designed for military purposes, won the favour of the Hungarian military leadership. Under the guidance of the HTI, the engineers of the Weiss Manfréd Factory utilised the A.C.2 armoured car chassis, Hungarian designed superstructure was constructed, which became the pre-type of the modern Hungarian armoured car.

The Hungarian armoured vehicle was given the license plate P-19, which was one of the Weiss Manfred Factory's test vehicles. Its hull differed significantly from the rounded version designed for the British vehicle. The A.C. Alvis superstructure designed for A.C.3 only became known in Csepel in 1938, so it is not known how much it affected the shape of the later 39 M. Csaba armoured car. The later Csaba turret was certainly formed here with small differences, and the arrangement of the weapon installation also became final.

In 1935, Straussler also designed a light artillery tractor and the prototype was produced by the Weiss Manfred Factory. It was planned to use by the British Army in mountainous terrain. It was transported to England in 1937 tested and used by the Alvis Company, probably destroyed by the Luftwaffe in Coventry during the war.

DESIGN AND DEVELOPMENT OF THE 39 M. CSABA ARMOURED CAR

The so-called Győri Program provided the financial background of the enlargement and modernisation of the Hungarian Army. It also focused on the creation of the armoured forces, equipping the country's Army with modern armoured vehicles. Implementation of the plan began with the production of 38 M. Toldi light tanks after the acquisition of the license rights to manufacture the L-60 tank from the Swedish Landsverk Factory.

The Hungarian Chief of Staff first tried to procure armoured cars through foreign purchases. The Austrian ADKZ, the Swedish Lynx and some German armoured vehicles seemed to be the right type, but - as in the case of tanks - the high purchase price, precarious international situation and the German reluctance to sell complicated the business.

Simultaneously with the foreign procurement, the Weiss Manfréd Factory submitted its production offer based on an armoured car in its possession. It was the prototype of the A.C. armoured car designed by Nicholas Straussler and the engineers of the Weiss Manfred Company.

The Weiss Manfréd's offer included the chassis, engine and running gear, but it also seemed suitable for construction with an armoured superstructure. The uncertainty surrounding foreign purchases, the deteriorating international situation, and the urgency of preparing for war forced the military leadership to accept the domestic production.

The A.C.2 with a Hungarian developed body, without turret and fenders, was tested as Borbála light artillery tractor for towing the 40mm Bofors autocannons, by the Hungarians but was more expensive than the Ford-Marmon trucks. (Sárhidai Gyula)

The A.C.2 armoured car with Hungarian made armoured hull and turret with A.012 number plate. The turret is already armed with one 20mm anti-tank rifle and one machine gun. A 31 M. light machine gun is on anti-aircraft mounting at the rear turret hatch. (Sárhidai Gyula)

The Hungarian A.C.2 armoured car at the workshop of the WM Factory during overturning test, on the left corner Ford engines are visible. (Fortepan/Korbuly)

Another photo of the A.C.2 armoured car was handed over to the Ludovika Military Academy for training. The rail antenna expands over the lengths of the rear hull. (Fortepan/Ludovika)

In the summer of 1938, the Hungarian Chief of Staff supporting the development of an indigenous armoured vehicle based on the A.C.2 armoured car design. The Weiss Manfréd Factory was commissioned to prepare the prototype. After operational trials with the prototype, in early 1939, the modified A.C.2 was adopted as a 39 M. Csaba striker armoured car, and by the end of the year, the production of the first series was ordered.

In the first phase of the construction of the armoured car, the A.C.2 first was used to test the vehicle's chassis, running gear, engine and transmission system. This test car was without a turret and fenders, with iron plates covering the hull. The rear-engine compartment was significantly higher than at the final version. The engine was cooled by a radiator on the back panel of the body. In cold weather, the grille could be closed with a linen cooling blanket.

After the first tests, the Factory built the final prototype. The body of the iron-riveted vehicle was modified in the engine compartment, with the rear plate attached to the cover at -8 °. The engine cooling opening was correspondingly lower, 7 baffles were installed. The muffler was mounted under the engine, on the outside, with a longer exhausting pipe bent backwards. The shape of the turret, the armament, and the location of the observation ports were already the same as the final embodiment, the only difference being the lower anchorage point of the anti-aircraft weapon stand, which was mounted under the tailgate, outside. There was a side door on the left side of the armoured hull, on the

A 39 M. Csaba and A.C.2 armoured cars parking next to each other at the yard of the Automobile Depot of the Army in 1943. The differences between the A.C.2 and the 39 M. Csaba is visible on the hull as well as on the turret. The A.C.2 also got the Pc.019 number plate, painted dark olive-green with white cross military insignia. (Fortepan/Lissák)

The 39 M. Csaba turrets were produced for the Hungarian River Forces, built on armoured minesweeper boats, called PAM in 1943. (Karai Sándor)

Test driving of the newly produced 39 M. Csaba armoured cars, du to the delays the turret was without weapons. The armoured cars were escorted by Factory and military personal. (Fortepan/Korbuly)

The half-rear view of the turret of the 39 M. Csaba armoured car, with opened rear doors, the observation ports visible inside the door. (Tóth Marcell)

The Pc.102 "iron" 39 M. Csaba training vehicle belongs to the 1st Reconnaissance Battalion, wearing the white lightning bolt unit sign painted on the right nose panel of the hull. (Mujzer Péter)

The 39 M. Csaba armoured cars were powered by a 90 hp Ford V-8 engine built in the rear of the armoured car. On the right side of the engine the Bosch battery is visible. (Fortepan/Korbuly)

The armoured hull of the Csaba consisted of riveted and bolted steel plates attached to the steel frame. The heptagonal frontal armour plate was removed by the mechanics to carry out the maintenance. (Móker József)

The front driver position with open driver cupola and steering wheel. On the right is one of the 31 M. carbine visible. Certain parts of the fighting compartment were padded to protect the crew. (Fortepan/Ludovika)

The machine gun installation of the 8mm 34/37 M. machine gun with the machine gun sight on the right side of the turret. On the left is the 20mm 36 M. anti-tank rifle between the weapons an observation port is visible. (Fortepan/Ludovika)

Turret weapons and the front driver position are visible in the photo. The internal steel frame structure is visible, which keep the bolted steel plates of the hull and turret. (Fortepan/Ludovika)

left side of the centre plate, to get the crew in and out, next to the turret hatches.

A prototype was made, formerly with registration number P-19, later license plate A-012, using a combination of frame and stick antennas. The stick antenna, when extended, prevented the turret from turning to the left. On the production vehicles, the stick antenna was used on the left side of the hull, built next to the turret, as the rear driver became responsible for operating the radio.

After testing with prototypes of the A.C.2, the 39 M. Csaba armoured car was built in its final form. The production unit price was 63,840 pengő (Hungarian currency) per vehicle. The armoured car has retained its basic characteristics - track width, wheelbase, wheel size, width, ground clearance, transmission and steering, etc. -, differences can be detected in the shape of the car body.

The prototype vehicle, A-012, made of iron plates, formally differs from A.C.2 listed below:

- The nose plate of the car became narrower and taller.
- The side edges of the front plate do not meet the edge point of the sidewall, only the front and side panels have been assembled by inserting two additional triangles.
- The side front door came forward on the left.
- The rear cover in the engine compartment has been steeper (-18 °), and the engine has been cooled by a vent at the top right of the cover.
- Instead of a folding assembly door, the necessary maintenance work could be carried out from the outside through circular mounting openings.
- The muffler was inside the car body.

Side view of the 39 M. Csaba armoured car, parking at the Automobile Depot of the Army in 1943, the authorised tire pressure, 4,0 atmosphere painted on the fenders. The turret weapons are in a protective canvas cover. (Fortepan/Lissák)

Rear view of the 39 M. Csaba armoured car with open rear turret hatch and driver's cupola, the interior of the armoured cars were painted white. The crew were officer candidates, belonged to the Ludovika Military Academy (Fortepan/Ludovika)

- The fenders did not protect the front wheels at all from the front, and smaller, replacement guards were fitted to protect the outer steering gear.
- The six-point-mounted frame antenna did not extend beyond the car body.
- The iron vehicles turret had a circular periscope socket located above the weapons' ports on the front plate, which is no longer found on later series armoured cars.

Based on the successful tests, the vehicle was put in service in 1939 as the 39 M. Csaba armoured car. At the same time, 61 vehicles were ordered from the Weiss Manfred Factory for the reconnaissance units.

When the 40 M. command version entered into service, the 39 M. was refered as striker version.

The serial copies were somewhat different from the prototype. The fenders, the nose and the tail were modified so that the moving wheels did not touch the body of the car when driving in the field. Engineers of the Weiss Manfred Factory, Ernő Kovácsházy and dr. Aurél Jurek redesigned the shape of the nose and tail and made all the modifications that they experimented with the A.C.2 armoured car.

The 39 M. Csaba armoured cars belonged to the 1st Reconnaissance Battalion in April 1941. Visible the frontal driver's cupola. The Pc.123 already had the octagonal military insignia. (Tálosi Zoltán)

Frontal view of the State Police Csaba armoured car, an observation port was installed instead of the anti-tank rifle, which was removed from the turret. A searchlight was attached to the left turret side. (Pálinkás Zsolt)

The overturned Pc.158 Csaba armoured car, the double-leaf springs are visible as well as the Cordatic spurn pattern tires. (Virág Ajtony)

The crew of the armoured car troops wearing the two-piece leather protective suit with Italian style 37M and 39 M. crash helmets. The 39 M. crash helmet had headphones for the commanders and radiomen. (Bonhardt Attila)

39 M. CSABA ARMOURED CAR

The Csaba had independent suspension, two and four-wheel drive, and four-wheel steering which could be set to front or rear two-wheel steering. These attributes gave the Csaba excellent off-road capabilities but required rather involved maintenance. The vehicle, which rode on four large 22x9,75 (1100 mm) tires, with servo air brakes was equipped with shot-resistant Cordatic tires, the suspension provided by two-two semi-elliptic leaf springs at front and rear. The relatively wide track width (1700 mm) and the 3000 mm wheelbase also resulted in stable road holding in the field. The armoured car was operated with a 90Hp V-8 German Ford engine positioned in the rear of the hull. The 90-horsepower, overdrive, 8-cylinder, in-line engine allowed the vehicle to move forward and backward with its 5-5-speed transmission system. The fuel was stored in a lower 120-litre fuel tank situated under the hull and a spare 15-litre fuel tank situated behind the rear armoured plate.

The hull of the Csaba armoured car was divided into driver, turret and engine compartment.

The Csaba's angularly-shaped body with no vertical plates was designed to give extra protection to the crew and engine by deflecting projectiles and shrapnel. The turret likewise was formed with angled armour plates. The armour of the vehicle, built of riveted and bolted armour plates, with a thickness of 13 mm on the front, 9 mm on the car body, and 7 mm on the cover plate. The vertical plates of the driver's cupola were also made with 13mm armour. The turret had 9mm armour plates too.

The 40 M. Csaba command/signal armoured cars employed as company and battalion command/signal armoured cars at the reconnaissance battalions. Factory fresh 40 M. armoured cars perform a test drive. (Fortepan/Korbuly)

On the hull of the armoured car, at front and rear, mudguards were fixed which provided space for storage boxes, entrenching tools, jacks. The armoured car had two driver's seats with the same control panels at the front and rear of the car, although the rear driver's seat was very narrow and squeezed to the left due to the engine situated at the rear of the car. The drivers were protected by an armoured cupola (called a helmet) which could be opened and lowered according to the combat situation. The driver's seat was adjustable by the drivers while driving the car. With a closed driving cupola, the drivers orientated through periscopes.

At the front driving position, ammunition boxes were attached to the walls for the anti-tank rifle, on the right side with 10 magazines, on the left 8 magazines and two 31 M. carbines.

The turret space in the hull accommodated the turret crew, ammunition boxes for the anti-tank rifle and the machine gun, repair kits, spare sights, radio. The turret space accommodated ammunition boxes for 122 magazines for the machine gun, 14 magazines for the anti-tank rifle. On the left side of the hull, a side door was placed for the crew for out and boarding.

The Csaba armoured car had a hexagonal shape centrally-positioned turret that rotated 360°. The side plates of the turret got observation ports. The rear turret plate accommodated a large double door with two observation ports too. The turret also had a roof hatch for the commander. The frontal plate accommodated the weapons of the armoured car. The 34/37 M. machine gun and its sight were built in the right weapon port and the 36 M. anti-tank rifle and its sight in the left one.

ARMAMENT

The turret fitted with a 20mm 36 M. anti-tank rifle and an 8mm Gebauer 34/37 M. machine gun. Also on board was a removable 8mm Solothurn 31 M. light machine gun that could fire through the rear hatch of the turret as an anti-aircraft weapon. The vehicle carried 200 rounds for the anti-tank rifle and 3000 rounds for the machine guns.

The Hungarian 20mm 36 M. anti-tank rifle was based on the Swiss Solothurn S-18/100 design. Its muzzle velocity was 762m/s. The projectile, the Hungarian AP (armour-piercing) shell, could pierce 20mm armour angled at 60° from 100m, and 16mm of armour angled at 60° from 500m. The weapon had a five rounds magazine and could fire 10-20 rounds per minute.

The Hungarian 8mm 34/37 M. Gebauer machine gun had a 25 rounds magazine and fired 8x56mmR ammunition. The 8mm Solothurn 31 M. light machine gun also fired 8x56mmR ammunition. Its magazine held 25 rounds, and the weapon's rate of fire was a moderate 350 rounds per minute.

Every crew member had a 9mm 37 M. service pistol for self-defence, two 8mm 31 M. carbines and hand grenades were stored too. Later, 35 M. rifles and 39 and 43 M. sub-machine guns were added to the weaponry.

SIGNAL EQUIPMENT

The 39 M. Csaba armoured car was equipped with an R/4 radio which operated using a frame antenna mounted outside the car body and a telescopic stick antenna built into the rear armour on the left side of the turret. It was operated by the rear driver/radioman.

CREW

It was manned by a crew of four comprising commander, gunner, front driver, and rear driver/radio operator. The Csaba had a tight fighting compartment especially when the crew wearing their leather protective suits. However, according to battlefield records, the Csaba armoured cars regularly evacuated their comrades from the damaged vehicles cramped six to eight men into their armoured cars.

MODIFICATIONS

The Csaba armoured vehicles were subjected to intense use on poor quality Transylvanian roads, and several construction defects surfaced in 1940. There was a massive crack at the steering house due to the weakness of the casting. The bulletproof tires were also 40 kilograms heavier than the inflated ones used during the trial run. Finally, the Hungarian Cordatic Factory's "spur" pattern, the ordinary inflated tire was used, because in practice it has been proven that the armoured cars can do a few kilometres even with damaged tires.

Steering the armoured vehicles required serious physical effort from the drivers, especially on the field. Due to its high degree of transmission at the steering, the vehicle was "lazy" and this often led to the car overturning in sharp turns. To avoid such problems, the Weiss Manfred Factory developed a compressed air power steering system at the steering mechanism, which made large transmissions unnecessary, thus making it easier to drive the vehicle. This steering gear change was replaced on all returned armoured cars during factory overhauls.

The engine was supplied with air through the fighting compartment; this also meant a large influx of dust during the movements - which in turn jeopardized the operation of the turret weapons. The crew also experienced in Transylvania that this air supply system "provided" a very unpleasant cold in the fighting compartment during the cooler autumn weather. To solve this, the Factory designed an air duct on the right side of the vehicle, which ensured that the cooling air was led directly to the engine. Due to this modification, the heat of the running engine provided the heating of the crew compartment.

The vehicle's commanders complained that due to the high engine noise, they could not control the drivers with verbal instructions. This was solved with a tube with a funnel. Later, in 1942 with the completed 40 M. Csaba command/radio vehicles, this was supplemented with an electric intercom system to ensure the transmission of commands, instructions and reports of the vehicle's commander.

A serious problem was that during the marches, the R/4 radio installed on the armoured cars provided only 20 kilometres range on flat and just 5 kilometres on mountainous terrain between the armoured cars and the higher command echelons. Even in telegraph mode, the connection was only able to double that, which still did not correspond with the 100 km range prescribed by the Hungarian Chief of Staff.

Therefore, there was a need for a "stand-alone company command/radio car" capable of providing a connection to the higher command at greater distances. This request was also submitted in June 1940 when another 32 Csaba armoured vehicles were ordered, of which 12 were already requested as command/signal versions

40 M. CSABA COMMAND/SIGNAL ARMOURED CAR

The Army ordered special designed command/signal vehicles, the 40 M. Csaba, for the reconnaissance units, which had a greater radio capacity. The main requirement for this model was to be very similar to the combat vehicle, to keep production simple and to avoid drawing special enemy attention to it. The HTI together with the WM Factory performed the task based on the standard 39 M. Csaba armoured car. The command vehicle received a smaller one-man turret with only one 8mm 34/37 M. Gebauer machine gun. To place the radios, the anti-tank rifle, its mountings and accessories fixed to the turret wall were removed from the turret. The fourth member of the crew became the radio operator instead of the gunner. For him, a seat was built between the driver's compartment and the turret. The commander was able to connect to all military radios at 100 km in RH telegraph mode and 160 km on medium wave. This was ensured by a frame antenna attached to four pneumatic support legs which could be lifted and retract. Only a dozen were built officially, though it is likely that a few damaged 39 M. were converted to command vehicles during the war.

HUNOR ARMOURED CAR

During the war, the Hungarian Army intended to replace the Csaba armoured car with a better armed and armoured vehicle with better off-road capacity and low profile. It would be the Hunor armoured car, which unfortunately never left the design table, not even a prototype was built. The plans were ready by 1943, prepared by the engineers of the Weiss Manfred Factory, Ernő Kovácsházy, Aurél Jurek and Sándor Treplán. However, the Weiss Manfred Factory was overloaded by the ongoing tank production.

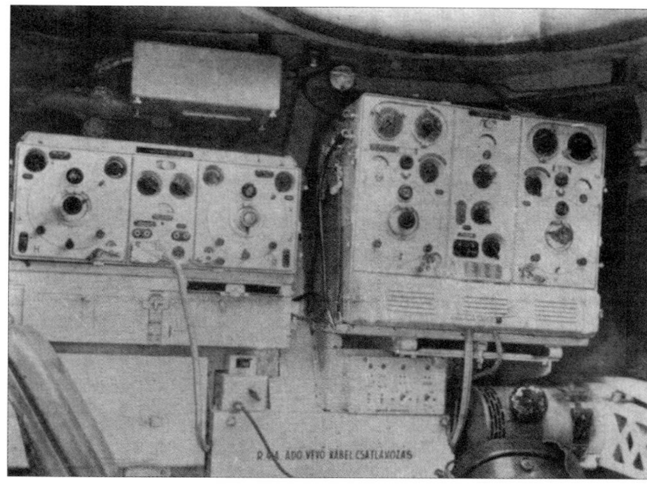

The 40 M. Csaba command/signal armoured car had one R/4T and two R/4 radios to communicate with subordinates and headquarters. (Service Manual)

The Ministry of Defence even reduced the third order of the Csaba armoured car from 70 to 50.

The hull was similar to the German Fu. Kfz.67/Kfz.232 armoured car, which was designed in 1935. The chassis was asymmetrical three-axle, six-wheel type, with 11.00 x 20 shoot resistant Lypsoid tire. This tire with a raw rubber inner tube was one of Straussler's patents, but during the war, the purchase of natural rubber was already hopeless. The drive was powered by two V-8 petrol engines with 165 hp. The armoured car had front and rear driving compartments. The turret of the armoured car is situated in the centre of the chassis, armed with one-one 20mm canon and 8mm machinegun, which was not too powerful at that time. It had a crew of 3-4. The armoured car had two propellers at the rear of the chassis, could switch to amphibious mode, the flotation was provided by a rubberized hose attached to the side of the armoured car inflated by compressed air. According to some theories, the plans of the Hunor armoured car got out of the Weiss Manfred Factory, reached England via Straussler in 1946. Utilised by Alvis Company at the Alvis-Straussler 12 tones Armoured Car, AAC 10-12 (DD type). Later, in 1949 used at the developments of Saladin and Saracen armoured cars too.

The 40 M. Csaba command/signal armoured cars had a smaller one-man turret. The frame antenna on pneumatic legs had two positions, elevated and lowered one. (Bonhardt Attila)

The 39 M. and 40 M. Csaba armoured cars had two frontal, circular hatches for the search lights, situated on the hull. The 40 M. series started with Pc.400 number plate. (Fortepan/Korbuly)

The Pc.410 command/signal armoured car advancing with its frame antenna in an elevated position. In difficult, forested terrain the frame antenna could be lowered. (Fortepan/Korbuly)

Technical Data

Designation: 39 M. Csaba striker armoured car

Years of production: 1939 – 1943
Factory: Weis Manfred Factory
Combat weight: 5.95 t
Length: 4520 mm
Width: 2100 mm
Height: 2370 mm
The wheelbase of 1.7m
Crew: 4
Engine: Ford G61T
Displacement: 3560 cm/3
Type Eight-cylinder, water-cooled
Fuel Petrol
Horsepower: 90-95 Hp
Speed: 65 km/h
The fuel tank capacity was 135 litres
Suspension Transverse semi-elliptic leaf springs
Range: 150-200 km
Obstacle crossing
crossing ditch: 0,5 m
fording depth of 1m
ability to climb a 30° slope
Armament: one 20mm 36 M. anti-tank rifle;
one 8mm 34/37 AM. machine-gun;
one 8mm 31 M. light machine-gun
Ammunition: 200 20mm shells
3000 8 mm machinegun cartridges
Armour: 9-13mm
Radio: R/4 with rail and stick antenna

Designation: 40 M. Csaba command/signal armoured car

Years of production: 1940 -1943
Factory: Weis Manfred Factory
Combat weight: 5.85 t
Length: 4520 mm
Width: 2100 mm
Height: 2300 mm
The wheelbase of 1.7m
Crew: 4
Engine: Ford G61T
Displacement: 3560 cm/3
Type Eight-cylinder, water-cooled
Fuel Petrol
Horsepower: 90-95 Hp
Speed: 70km/h
The fuel tank capacity was 135 litres
Suspension Transverse semi-elliptic leaf springs
Range: 150-200 km
Obstacle crossing
crossing ditch: 0,5 m
fording depth of 1m
ability to climb a 30° slope
Armament: one 8mm 34/37 AM. machine-gun
Ammunition: 4000 8 mm machine gun cartridges
Armour: 9-13mm
Radio: one R/4a, two R/4 with a frame antenna

A post-war experimental light armoured car prototype, the similarity to the Csaba armoured cars are noticeable. The program was cancelled due to the arriving Soviet armament in the late 40s. (Sárhidai Gyula)

PRODUCTION

The Csaba armoured cars were exclusively produced by Weiss Manfred Factory at Csepel, in one of the suburb of the Hungarian capital. The number of armoured cars manufactured since 1939 is mentioned differently by various sources - between 93 and 172 were made. According to the production reports of the Weiss Manfred Factory, the first three 39 M. Csaba armoured cars were handed over to the troops in January 1940.

The Weiss Manfred Factory made the first 8 vehicles (with license plates Pc.101 to 108) with iron plate superstructure, as it did not receive enough armour plates in time. These were used as training vehicles at the armoured car companies, to speed up the training. The prototype, the A.C.2 armoured car, which was owned by the Weiss Manfred Factory in 1940 was also transferred to the Army. It had an iron plate superstructure, unsuitable for combat use, but suitable for training. It ended as a target at an artillery range and was demolished in 1943.

In April 1940, the units had 8 iron/training and 15 steel plated cars, and by 20 June 1940, the numbers have grown to 8 iron and 54 armoured cars (Pc.101-Pc.163). The photo evidence proved that a 39 M. Csaba armoured car with number plate Pc.163 took part in the operation in Transylvania.

At the time of the war against the Soviet Union in 1941, three reconnaissance battalions were sent to the front with 48 armoured cars. Compensating the lost armoured cars, 9 additional 39 M. Csaba was sent to the front. So, in addition to the 8 iron/training vehicles, 57 were available in 1941.

According to the new researches, four battalions, the 1st and 2nd Reconnaissance and the 1st and 2nd Armoured Cavalry Battalions fought in Ukraine. However, the 2nd Armoured Cavalry Battalion only fought in the first months of the operation. It means that theoretically, the four companies had 4x18 altogether 72 39 M. and 40 M. Csaba armoured cars. But most likely the armoured car companies were not on full strength. Due to the operations, 80% of the deployed Csaba armoured cars were broken, damaged or knocked out, but shipped back to Hungary for repair.

In 1942, the Weiss Manfred Factory only carry out the factory overhaul of the damaged and broken armoured vehicles. During factory overhaul, some combat vehicles were converted into 40 M. Csaba signal/command armoured cars, like the Pc.162 and Pc.182 armoured cars.

During the deployment of the 2nd Hungarian Army to the Eastern Front, the 1st Reconnaissance Battalion had 18 39 M. and 40 M. Csaba armoured cars, the known number plates were Pc.125, 137, 138, 147, 175 and 183.

The following orders have been issued to the Weiss Manfred Factory by the Army.

1st order was 61 39 M. armoured cars in 1939.

2nd order was 32 39 M. armoured cars in 1940.

3rd order was 70 39 M. armoured cars in 1941.

Ministry of Interior ordered two modified 39 M. armoured cars for the State Police in 1940. These police armoured cars were delivered without the standard military weaponry. The armament consisted only one machine gun, instead of the anti-tank rifle an observation port was installed. So far no information existing about the exact type of the machine gun, but analysing the photo evidences, the armoured cars were not armed with the 8mm 34/37 AM. machine guns. Most likely that the old 07 M. Schwarzlose machine guns, previously used in the Vickers armoured cars were installed in the turrets.

According to the distributed number plates the next armoured cars were produced and handed over to the armoured car companies:

- Pc.101-108 iron/training vehicles
- Pc.109-161 53 39 M. Csaba armoured cars
- Pc.163-181 19 39 M. Csaba armoured cars
- Pc.182-192 11 39 M. Csaba armoured cars
- Pc.162 and Pc.182 converted to 40 M. Csaba command/signal armoured car
- Pc.400-411 12 40 M. Csaba command/signal armoured car

These delivered vehicles belonged to the first and second-order of the Ministry of Defence. According to the records the first and second orders were fulfilled by the end of 1941. In 1943, the Ministry of Defence ordered 20 complete 39 M. Csaba turrets for the River Forces. These were intended to build into the Armoured Patrol (PM) and Armoured Minesweeper Boats (PAM) in 1944. The handover of 18 turrets was documented in March 1944. According to technical drawings, one old river patrol boat was also armed with one 39 M. Csaba turret, it was installed on the top of the armoured conning tower.

From the third order which from 70 was reduced to 50 armoured cars, only 12 armoured cars were completed. The highest known number plate of the 39 M. Csaba armoured car according to the production records was Pc.192, the highest known number plate on photos was Pc.183. This suggests that the Weiss Manfred Factory started the production of the third order of the Ministry of Defence using the already available parts and components. By 14 July 1944, the Weis Manfred Factory reported 6 39 M. and 6 40 M. armoured cars ready to the Ministry of Defence with missing bits and parts. These were; the Pc.193-198, 6 39 M. Csaba armoured cars and the Pc.412-417, 6 40 M. Csaba command/signal armoured cars. According to the instruction of the Ministry of Defence on 04 July, these vehicles were handed over to the troops. The missing parts were later installed at the units. Until the Allied bomb raid of the Weiss Manfred Factory on 27 July 1944, 11 more 39 M. Csaba armoured car was produced with the possible highest number plate of Pc.198. The final numbers of the 40 M. Csaba command/signal armoured cars not know, 20 confirmed and probably two more was built.

According to the reports the Weiss Manfred Factory built 97 39 M. Csaba armoured cars and 20 40 M. Csaba command/signal armoured cars plus probably two more, altogether 119 armoured cars. After the war, 20 unfinished Csaba armoured car bodies were found in the yard of the Weiss Manfred Factory in the summer of 1945.

An interesting after war episode connected to the designer, Nicolaus Straussler, who forwarded a license fee claim against the Weis Manfred Factory in 1946. Straussler claimed his fee based on the production of 172 armoured cars. This list listed 99 armoured cars, 18 command/signal armoured cars, 2 police armoured cars and 53 export variants. This was rejected shortly by the new owners of Weiss Manfred Factory.

39 M. Csaba armoured cars advancing on dirt roads in Transylvania September 1940. The vehicles had a three-tone camouflage but no military insignia probably belonged to the 2nd Armoured Cavalry Battalion. (Gőgh Gábor)

The reconnaissance and armoured cavalry battalions almost had same the organisation during the operation in Transylvania in 1940, each had one-one armoured car company with ten 39 M. Csaba armoured cars. (Mujzer collection)

THE ORGANISATION OF THE ARMOURED CAR TROOPS OF THE RECONNAISSANCE UNITS

EARLY ORGANISATION

In 1938 the newly created motorised brigades each had one (armoured) reconnaissance battalion. The reconnaissance battalion of the 2nd Brigade was the first armour unit of the Hungarian Army with one – one armoured car, tankette and motorised rifle companies. The strength of the unit was based on the 3rd and 4th Tankette Companies and the armoured cars of the Experimental Mechanised Group. Later, the armoured units of the cavalry brigades were enlarged to battalion size similar to the armoured battalions of the motorised brigades, consisting of one company each of light tanks, tankettes and armoured cars. The armoured car companies had 10 vehicles; three platoons each with 3 armoured vehicles plus the company commander's vehicle.

As of December 1940, the Mobile Corps order of battle was re-organised following the delivery of the new 38 M. Toldi light tanks and 39 M. Csaba armoured cars in significant quantity. The organisation of the new tank battalions started, one-one bicycle battalions were converted to tank units at both motorised brigades. It had an impact on the reconnais-

Armoured car company of the 1st Reconnaissance Battalion during the occupation of Transylvania, the company had 10 39 M. Csaba armoured cars together with the training vehicles. The unit had its own Maltese cross military insignia. (Szollár János)

Happy troopers of the 2nd Reconnaissance Battalion parking in a Transylvanian town. The 39 M. Csaba armoured cars fresh from the factory had missing parts, for example, the armoured car on the left had no rail antenna. (Mujzer Péter)

The terrain and the roads were demanding in Transylvania, the Pc.145 39 M. Csaba armoured car and 35M Fiat Ansaldo tankettes mixed with infantry and pack animals. (Fortepan)

sance battalions too. According to the new organisation, the reconnaissance battalion had a one-one armoured car, motorcycle, motorised rifle and anti-tank companies and one-one signal, sapper and maintenance platoons subordinated to the battalion staff. The armoured car company had 16 x 39 M. and 40 M. armoured cars, organised into three platoons, each had 5 armoured cars and one 40 M. Csaba command/signal armoured car belonged to the company staff. The anti-tank gun company had 4x 37mm 36 M (Pak36) anti-tank guns. The motorised rifle company had 12 x 8mm 31 M. Solothurn light machine guns, 2 x 50mm 39 M. light mortars, 2 x 20mm 36 M. Solothurn anti-tank rifles. The motorcycle company was armed with 12 x 8mm 31 M. Solothurn light machine guns, 2 x 20mm 36 M. Solothurn anti-tank rifles.

The cavalry brigades had one-one armoured cavalry battalions with one armoured car company with 16 x 39 M. Csaba armoured cars, two tankette companies with 35 M. FIAT Ansaldo tankettes, one anti-tank gun company with 37mm 36M anti-tank guns and one-one signal, sapper and maintenance platoons subordinated to the battalion staff. The armoured cavalry battalions were also reinforced with 10 x 38 M. Toldi light tanks.

The 1st Hungarian Mountain Brigade also had one armoured car platoon in 1941. The armoured car platoon had

Assembled units of the 2nd Cavalry Brigade, at the front a bicycle battalion lined with its tanket platoon and motorised howitzer battery. In the background is the 2nd Armoured Cavalry Battalion with its armoured car company. (Fortepan)

39 M. Csaba armoured cars belonged to the 2nd Armoured Cavalry Battalion with octagonal military insignia took part in the Yugoslavian operation in April 1941. (Móker József)

The 1st Mountain Brigade had one armoured car platoon with three 39 M. Csaba armoured cars in 1941. The unit sign was the white 1.hgy. (War Correspondent Company)

22 men 3 x 39 M. Csaba an armoured car, two motorcycles and one-one staff car and truck. The armoured car platoon was disbanded by the end of 1941.

In 1942 an ad-hoc unit, the 1st Armoured Field Division was organised and sent to the front. The 1st Reconnaissance Battalion was incorporated into the Field Division, its organisation already reflected on the lessons learned during the Barbarossa Campaign in 1941.

The 1st Reconnaissance Battalion had one motorised rifle company (12 x 8mm 31 M. Solothurn light machine guns, 2 x 50mm 39 M. light mortars, 2 x 20mm 36 M. Solothurn anti-tank rifles), one motorcycle company (12 x 8mm 31 M. Solothurn light machine guns, 2 x 20mm 36 M. Solothurn anti-tank rifles), one anti-tank gun company (4 x 37mm 36M, 2 x 50mm Pak38 anti-tank guns), one armoured car company. The armoured car company had three platoons, each consisting of 4 x Csaba armoured cars, one-one 40 M. Csaba command/signal armoured car belonged to the company and battalion staff. The strength of the reconnaissance battalion consisted of 26 officers, 42 NCO and 503 men, equipped with 102 solo and side-car motorbikes, 5 Mercedes G5 command cars, 56 trucks, among them 37 38M Botond trucks, 4 Krupp Protze anti-tank gun tractors, 8 Ford-Marmon trucks, one-one workshop and R/7 signal trucks. By that time the squad, platoon and company commanders were armed with 9mm German MP-40 sub-machine guns.

FINAL ORGANISATION

Two different type reconnaissance battalion was organised, one for the new infantry divisions and one for the armoured and cavalry divisions.Following the new overall organisation, the Hungarian Army had eight first-line infantry divisions (each with three infantry regiments) and each of them had one assault gun battalion and one reconnaissance battalion.

Reconnaissance battalions at the infantry divisions

The reconnaissance battalions belonging to the eight first-line infantry divisions consisted of one hussar and one

An armoured car platoon with five 39 M. Csaba armoured cars and the supply tail with Ford trucks. The turrets had camouflaged protective canvas cover. (Szollár jános)

39 M. Csaba armoured car, Pc.144 belonged to the armoured car company of the 1st Armoured Cavalry Battalion in Ukraine 1941, the unit sign painted on the turret, above the machine gun port. (Mujzer collection)

40 M. Csaba command/signal armoured cars were employed as company and battalion commander's vehicles from 1941, the Pc.401 belonged to the 2nd Armoured Cavalry Battalion. (Móker József)

bicycle company, and one platoon each of armoured cars (4 x 39 M. Csaba armoured cars), anti-tank gun (4 x 40mm 40 M. or 75mm 43 M./Pak40 anti-tank guns), mortar (4 x 81mm 36 M. mortars), signal and sapper. The armoured car platoons were rarely equipped with armoured cars due to the shortage of the 39 M. Csaba armoured cars.

Reconnaissance battalions at the 1st and 2nd Armoured Divisions

The two armoured divisions also had one reconnaissance battalions each. The 1st Reconnaissance Battalion was stationed at Budapest, the 2nd Reconnaissance Battalion based at Kassa (Kosice) wearing the tactical numbers of their armoured divisions. These reconnaissance battalions were equipped with an armoured car company, a motorised rifle company (12 x 8mm 31 M. Solothurn light machine guns, 2 x 50mm 39 M. mortars, 2 x 20mm 36M. Solothurn anti-tank rifles), a motorcycle company (12 x 8mm 31 M. Solothurn light machine guns, 2 x 20mm 36 M. Solothurn anti-tank rifles), anti-tank gun company (4 x 40mm 40 M. or 75mm 43 M./Pak 40 anti-tank guns), the battalion staff had one-one signal, sapper, maintenance platoons. The armoured car company had three platoons each had 4 x 39 M. Csaba armoured cars, one-one 40 M. Csaba armoured command/signal car served at the company staff and the battalion HQ.

Reconnaissance battalion at the 1st Cavalry Division

The 1st Cavalry Division included the 3rd Reconnaissance Battalion; its peacetime garrison was at Szilágysomlyó. The battalion had two armoured car companies with 26 x 39 M. Csaba armoured cars, and one anti-tank company (4 x 40mm 40 M. or 75mm 43 M./Pak 40 anti-tank guns), the battalion staff had one-one signal, sapper and maintenance platoons. The armoured car companies had three platoons each had 4 x 39 M. Csaba armoured cars, one-one 40 M. Csaba armoured command/signal car served at the company staff and the battalion HQ. The armoured cars of the two former armoured cavalry battalions were concentrated in the new 3rd Reconnaissance Battalion, although it did not gain full strength until 1944.

39 M. Csaba armoured car in static observation position with light machine gun team armed with an 8mm 31 M. light machine gun and 35 M. rifles. (War Correspondent Company)

PARAMILITARY ORGANISATIONS WITH ARMOURED CARS

Gendarmerie

A gendarmerie battalion was formed at Galánta in 1942, which was responsible for internal security, against armed riots; it had three rifle companies, one bicycle company, one heavy weapons company and one armoured company. In 1944 the Gendarmerie Armoured Company had twelve 35 M. FIAT Ansaldo tankettes and one platoon of 39 M. Csaba armoured cars.

State Police

As of 1942, the mobile reserve of the State Police was also equipped with armoured vehicles. An armoured group was organised with ten 35 M. FIAT Ansaldo tankettes and two (according to some sources five) 39 M. Csaba armoured cars and a special storm detachment to keep internal order in the capital. The armoured car and tankett subunits were lead by officers. The 39 M. Csaba armoured car was just armed with the 8mm machinegun, the 20mm anti-tank rifle was removed. The armoured vehicles were painted dark blue.

OPERATIONAL HISTORY

The armoured car units took part in all major Hungarian military operations during the war. The armoured car companies were organised into the reconnaissance/ armoured cavalry battalions of the Mobile Troops and later also belonged to reconnaissance battalions of the new infantry divisions from 1943. Besides the early operations of 1938-1939, the armoured car companies were exclusively equipped with the Hungarian designed and produced 39 M. and 40 M. Csaba armoured cars.

1939 Trans-Carpathian Ukraine

The reconnaissance and armoured cavalry battalions were lack of armoured cars and light tanks at that time. In January 1939, the 2nd Reconnaissance Battalion had one-one tankett, light tank and armoured car company, which only had one Crossley, two Vickers armoured cars, temporarily reinforced with one captured ex-Czech Tatra OA vz. 30 armoured car.

1940 Transylvania

The armoured cavalry and reconnaissance battalions had received their 39 M. Csaba armoured cars at the assembly areas only at the last minute. The factory-fresh vehicles were incomplete and had a lot of mechanical failures. The military occupation of Northern Transylvania was carried out from 5 to 13 of September. The poor state of the roads created many mechanical problems for the mobile forces. Ten 39 M. Csaba armoured cars of the 1st Motorised Brigade had broken down by the end of the peaceful operation, due to the bad roads and weak construction of the vehicles.

1941 Yugoslavian Campaign

That time the mobile troops were organising the new tank battalions. Due to the slowness of mobilisation and a lack of armaments, the units were not at full strength. For example, the 2nd Motorised Brigade lacked 10 light tanks and 8 armoured cars, 135 motorcycles and 21 miscellaneous wheeled vehicles. However, the 39 M. Csaba armoured cars led the advancing Mobile troops during the short campaign.

The 1st Reconnaissance Battalion was deployed as the forward element of the 1st Motorised Brigade. During the night of 11 April, three reconnaissance groups were formed and deployed in the area of Hercegszántó. The 1st Armoured Cavalry Battalion (one company each of armoured cars, light tanks and tankettes) was reinforced with a light howitzer battery.

39 M. Csaba armoured car belonged to the 2nd Reconnaissance Battalion, battalion staff advancing in Transylvania September 1940. The white 2.F. was the unit sign, the T. stands for staff. Behind the armoured car is an ex-Polish Polski-Fiat 508 staff car. (War Correspondent Company)

The armoured car company of the 2nd Armoured Cavalry Battalion was equipped with 39 M. Csaba armoured cars crossing a 33 M. military bridge during the occupation of Transylvania. (Fortepan)

The battalions started their advance on the afternoon of 11 April. The armoured car and light tank companies reached the Serb fortifications, which were abandoned. The 2nd Armoured Cavalry Battalion also arrived at abandoned Serb positions at Bajmok-East.

The 2nd Cavalry Brigade sent 39 M. Csaba armoured cars under 1st Lieutenant László Béldy on 13 April, to explore the stronghold at Szenttamás (Srbobran). He was the company commander of the Armoured Car Company of 2nd Armoured Cavalry Battalion; he led his company towards Szenttamás when he noticed that the combat formation of his armoured car company became clumsy. He stopped the Company and ordered the troops to keep the proper formation. After this short stop, the Armoured Car Company continued with 1st Lieutenant Béldi's Csaba armoured car leading the company. A well-camouflaged 37mm Serbian anti-tank gun opened up on the advancing 39 M. Csaba armoured cars, the Pc.109 was hit five times, the Pc.118 was shot three times. 1st Lieutenant Béldi and his five men were killed, just two survived. Posthumously he was decorated with the Hungarian Knight Cross with swords. The vehicles were later repaired.

Barbarossa Campaign 1941

Under the new organisation, the motorised rifle brigades had one light tank and one reconnaissance battalion, and the cavalry brigades had one armoured cavalry battalion. The largest number of Csaba armoured cars was organised into four companies and one platoon took part in the Barbarossa Campaign in the summer-autumn of 1941. Although, the armoured car company of the 2nd Armoured Cavalry Battalion was only deployed for a short period.

39 M. Csaba armoured cars of the 2nd Armoured Cavalry Battalion, the armoured cars just arrived at the troops in summer of 1940, no military insignia was painted on the hull, small national flags and flowers attached to the hull. (Fortepan/Csorba)

The Pc.124 Csaba belonged to the 1st Reconnaissance Battalion, wearing the Maltese cross military insignia painted on the turret and on the hull side too, in front of the 39 M. Csaba armoured car is a 37mm 36 M. anti-tank gun visible. (Fortepan)

39 M. Csaba armoured car, 1st Reconnaissance Battalion entering a liberated Transylvanian town, the commander wearing the distinctive 39 M. crash helmet with headphone set. (Szollár János)

Hungarian civilians greeted the armoured car patrol of the 1st Reconnaissance Battalion in Voivodina, April 1941. The 39 M. Csaba armoured car still wearing the Maltese cross insignia and the white lightning bolt unit sign. (Szollár János)

Lined up armoured car company led by a Mercedes G5 company commander car. The 39 M. Csaba armoured cars already had the octagonal military insignia, probably belonged to the 1st Armoured Cavalry Battalion. (Deák Tamás)

Hungarian staff major observing the half-finished Yugoslavian fortifications in 1941, at the bottom is an armoured car Pc.185, an original 39 M. armoured car rebuilt as 40 M. Csaba armoured command/signal car. (Fortepan/Korbuly)

The Pc.155 39 M. Csaba armoured car belonged to the 1st Reconnaissance Battalion hit by a land mine in a village at Voivodina, April 1941. The turret is covered with camouflaged canvas to protect the vehicle. (Fortepan)

Overturned 39 M. Csaba armoured car of the 1st Reconnaissance Battalion during the Yugoslavian Campaign in April 1941. The weapons were already removed from the turret.

On 13 April 1941, the reconnaissance detachment of the 2nd Armoured Cavalry battalion was ambushed at Szenttamás. The Pc.109 was shot by 5 times by a 37mm Yugoslavian anti-tank gun. (Markó Ferenc)

The Pc.118 was hit 3 times by the same 37mm Yugoslavian anti-tank gun. 1st Lieutenant László Béldi and five of his crew were killed, just two men survived, most probably the rear drivers. (Markó Ferenc)

The battalion staff of one of the reconnaissance battalion taking a short rest on the way to the assembly area at the Carpathian Mountains. The column was led by a mobilised civilian Opel Kapiten car, followed by a 40 M. Csaba command/signal armoured car, a 39 M. Csaba armoured car and Ford-Marmon trucks. (Markó Ferenc)

Armoured car platoon in the Carpathian Mountains in early July 1941. The number plate Pc.180 is painted on a white square background. The crew was just armed with 9mm 37 M. service pistols for self-defence. (Szollár János)

Maintenance and washing of the 39 M. Csaba armoured cars belonged to the armoured car platoon of the 2nd Armoured Cavalry Battalion in July of 1941. The 2nd Armoured Cavalry Battalion took part in the initial operation, soon subordinated to the VIII. Corps. (War Correspondent Company)

39 M. Csaba armoured car belonged to the Armoured Car Platoon of the 1st Mountain Brigade, trying to overcome the difficult terrain in the Carpathian Mountain, helped by the troops. (Mujzer collection)

Burned out 39 M. Csaba armoured car, P.125 belonged to the 1st Reconnaissance Battalion, shot out at Rogozna in July 1941. (Szollár János)

The turret and the tire of the Pc.132 were shot in the summer of 1941; the seriously damaged vehicles were collected and sent back to Hungary for repair. The 39 M. Csaba armoured car belonged to the 2nd Reconnaissance Battalion, still wearing the circular military insignia. (Mujzer collection)

Due to the demolished bridges the reconnaissance patrol of the 1st Armoured Cavalry Battalion, two 39 M. Csaba armoured car and two 38 M. Botond truck crossing the River Dniester by a locally found ferry in early July 1941. (Mujzer collection)

Heavily camouflaged 39 M. Csaba armoured cars belonged to the 1st Armoured Cavalry Battalion advancing towards the encirclement of Uman. Next to the rear driver cupola, a white air identification panel was fixed. (War Correspondent Company)

Reserve 2nd Lieutenant László Merész, then ensign commanded the armoured car platoon of the 1st Armoured Cavalry Battalion, which repulsed the Soviet break trough attempt at Golovanevsk on 06 August 1941. (Illésfalvi Péter)

Hungarian soldiers examining the impact of a Soviet anti-tank shell on the turret of a knocked out 39 M. Csaba armoured car. The 9-17mm armour plates just protected against infantry weapons and splinters, even the Soviet anti-tank rifles could knock out the Csaba armoured cars. (Mujzer Péter)

39 M. Csaba armoured car belonged to the 1st Reconnaissance Battalion, wearing the unique, white heart platoon insignia, painted on the military insignia. Behind the armoured car is a Ford-Marmon four-wheel-drive truck visible. (Deák Tamás)

Painted by/Rysował: Arkadiusz Wróbel

40. M Csaba command/signal armoured car belonged to the 2nd Reconnaissance Battalion fought at Galicia in April 1944.

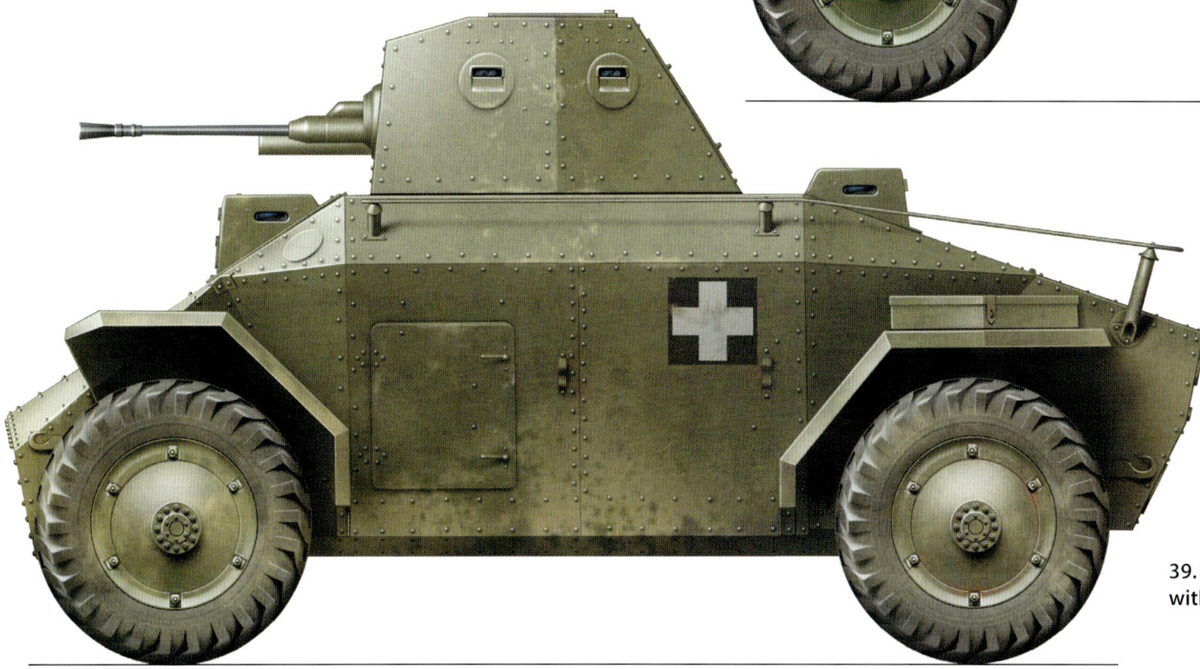

39. M Csaba armoured car have the standard olive green camouflage with late style military insignia, probably belonged to the armoured car company of one of the reconnaissance battalion.

39 M. Csaba armoured cars of the 2nd Reconnaissance Battalion during the operation in Transylvania, September 1940. The battalion had the circle size military insignia and the white F.2. unit sign stands for the 2nd Reconnaissance Battalion, the horizontal white bar represents the 1st Platoon of the Armoured Car Company. (Deák Tamás)

The 39 M. Csaba armoured cars of the 2nd Reconnaissance Battalion had three-tone camouflage and circle size military insignia in September 1940. (Deák Tamás)

38M Toldi light tanks and 39 M. Csaba armoured cars of the 1st Reconnaissance Battalion with three-tone camouflage and white lightning bolt unit sign during a summer exercise in 1941. (Deák Tamás)

Painted by/Rysował: Arkadiusz Wróbel

Prototype of 40 M. Csaba command/signal armoured car with three tone camouflage.

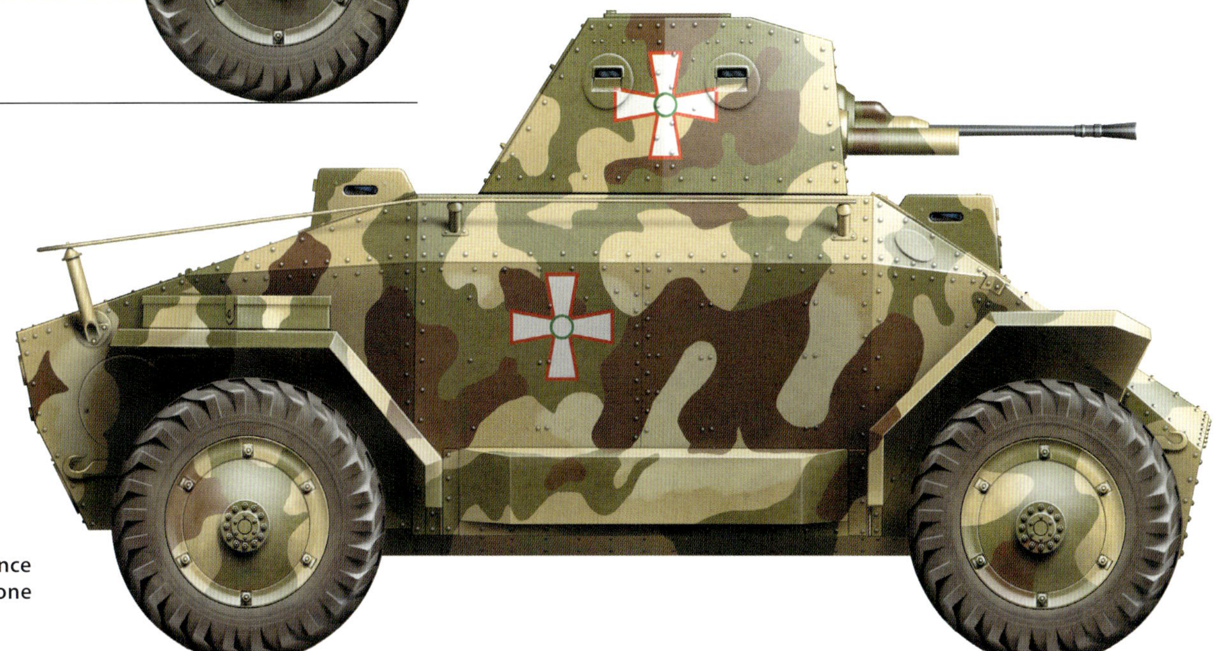

39. M Csaba armoured car belonged to the 1st Reconnaissance Battalion with Maltese cross military insignia and three tone camouflage, September 1940, occupation of Transylvania.

39. M Csaba armoured car with three tone camouflages and octagonal military insignia belonged to the Mobil Corps during the operation in Ukraine, summer of 1941.

39. M Csaba armoured car belonged to the armoured car company of the 2nd Reconnaissance Battalion wears the dark yellow camouflage, during the operation around Nadworna, April of 1944, Galicia.

1st Reconnaissance Battalion 1940-1941

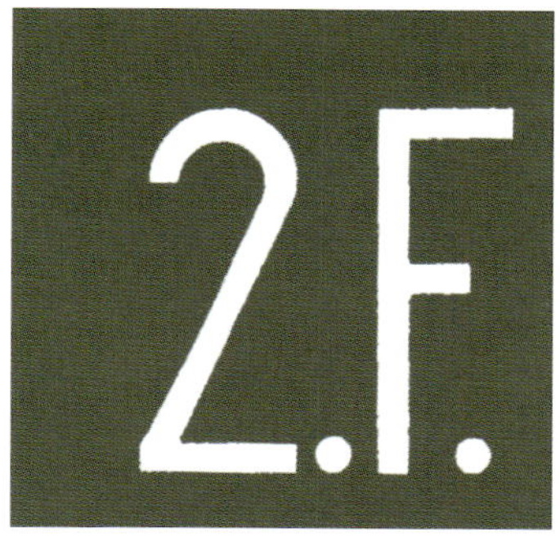

2nd Reconnaissance Battalion 1940-1941

1st Mountain Brigade, Armoured Car Platoon 1941

2nd Reconnaissance Battalion 1941?

1st Armoured Cavalry Battalion 1939-1941

1st Reconnaissance Battalion 1942-1945

2nd Reconnaissance Battalion 1942-1945

3rd Reconnaissance Battalion

1st Armoured Pioneer Battalion 1943-1945

Maltese cross insignia 1940

Circular insignia 1940-1941

Octagonal insignia 1941-1942

White cross-black square insignia 1943-1945

Mechanised Brach Sign insignia

Original German situation map about the German and Hungarian troops around Golovanevsk and Moldovka in early August of 1941 (HIM)

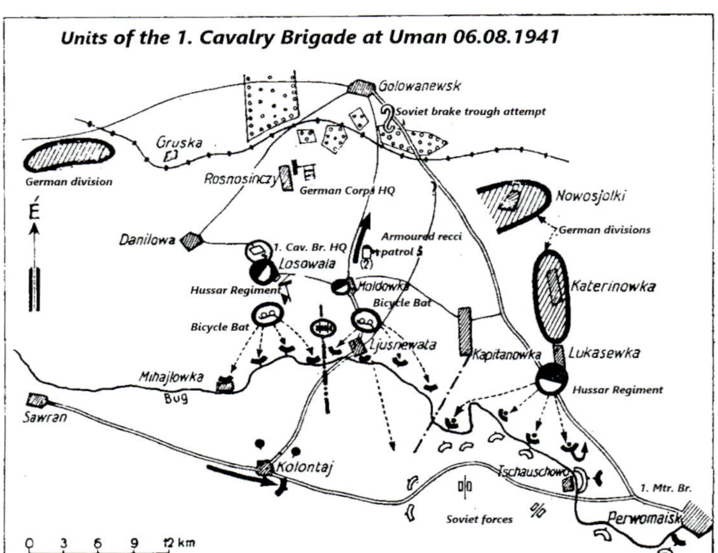

Hungarian maps about the location of the Hungarian Mobile Coprs, 1st Cavalry, 1st Motorised Brigades and German units on 06 August 1941, around Uman.

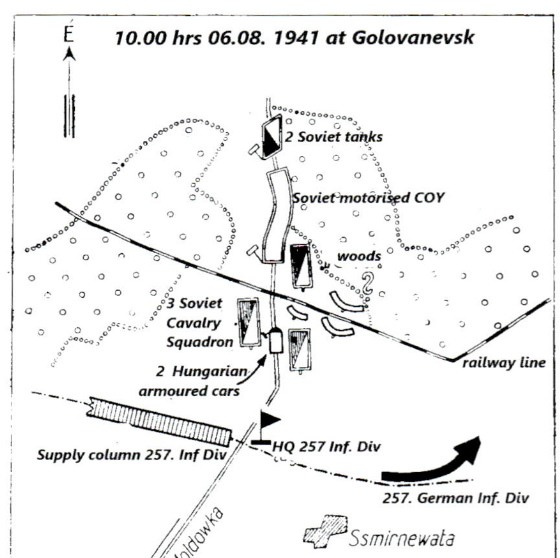

Situation map of the reconnaissance patrol of the 1st Cavalry Brigade led by Ensign László Merész around 10.00 hours, 06 August 1941.

Armoured car company of the 2nd Armoured Cavalry Battalion during the operation in Yugoslavia, April 1941. The 39 M. Csaba armoured cars were led by a Mercedes G5 command car. (Deák Tamás)

Advancing 39 M. Csaba armoured car of the 1st Reconnaissance Battalion at the Carpathian Mountains with octagonal military insignia. (Deák Tamás)

39 M. Csaba armoured car belonged to the 1st Armoured Reconnaissance Battalion in the summer of 1941, during the operation in Ukraine. (Deák Tamás)

Burned out 39 M. Csaba armoured car, Pc.125 belonged to the 1st Reconnaissance Battalion, July 1941. (Deák Tamás)

39 M. Csaba armoured car belonged to the 1st Armoured Reconnaissance Battalion in the summer of 1941, passing a bridge in the Carpathian Mountains. (Deák Tamás)

39 M. Csaba armoured car and a light machine gun team in a lookout position in Ukraine, summer of 1941. (Deák Tamás)

39 M. Csaba armoured car belonged to the 1st Armoured Cavalry Battalion wading a creek at the Carpathian Mountains. (Deák Tamás)

The original photo of the 39 M. Csaba armoured car belonged to the 1st Reconnaissance Battalion, wearing a white heart platoon sign painted into the octagonal military insignia.

Experimental 40 M. Csaba command/signal armoured car slipped into a ditch during the trial run, surrounded by factory crew, and Ford-Marmon truck. (Deák Tamás)

Sand-yellow camouflaged 39 M. Csaba armoured car belonged to the 2nd Reconnaissance Battalion, April 1944 Nadworna, Galicia. (Deák Tamás)

Color sectional drawing of the 39 M. Csaba armored car for training. (Service Manual)

39 M. Csaba armoured car with dark olive-green camouflage and white cross–black square military insignia, parking at the yard of the Automobile Depot in 1943. (Deák Tamás)

AC1 armoured car
Weiss Manfred

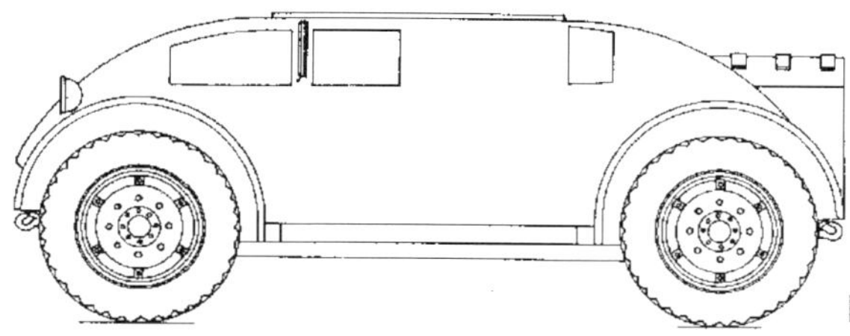

Borbála light artillery tractor
Weiss Manfred

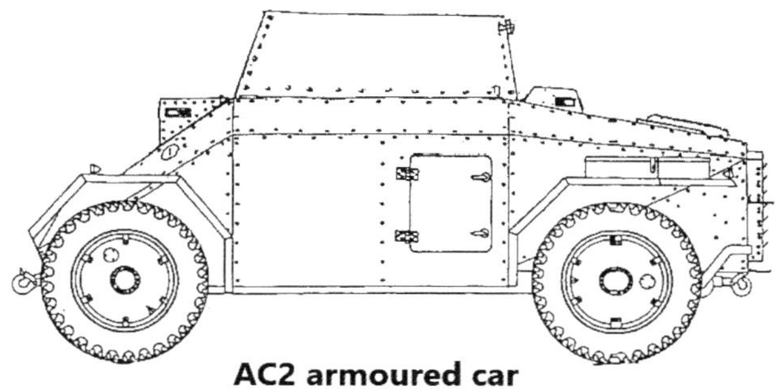

AC1 armoured car
Alvis Ltd

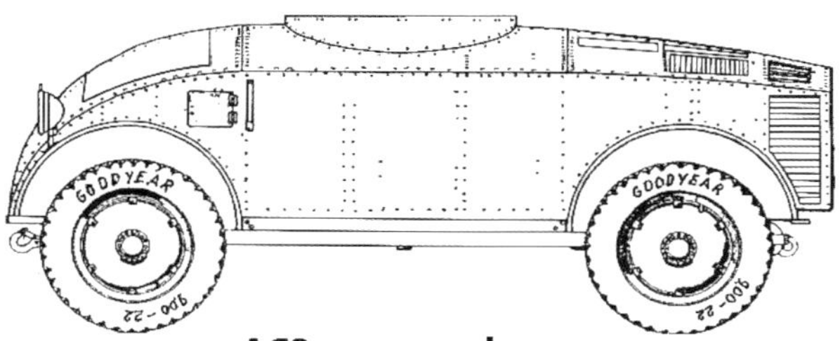

AC2 armoured car
Weiss Manfred

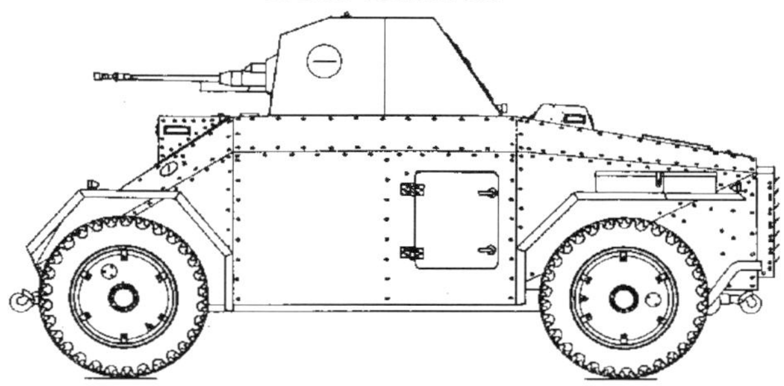

AC2 armoured car
British Army

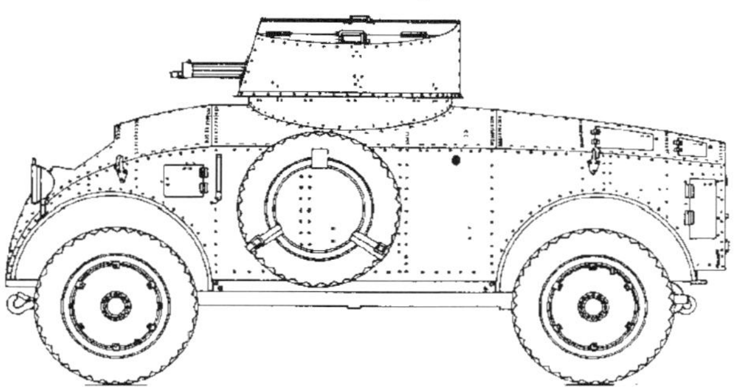

39M Csaba armoured car

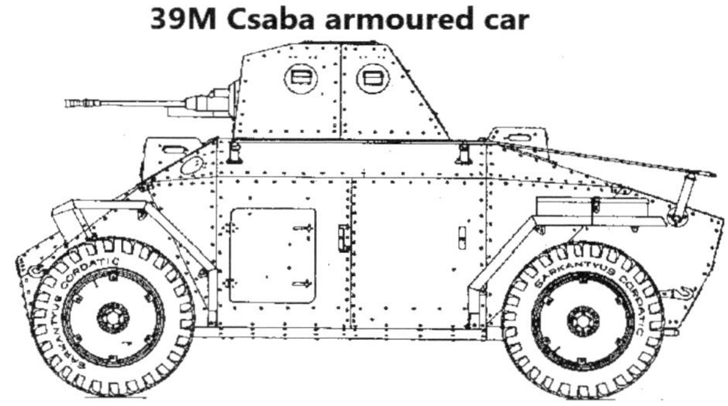

AC3D armoured car
Dutch Army

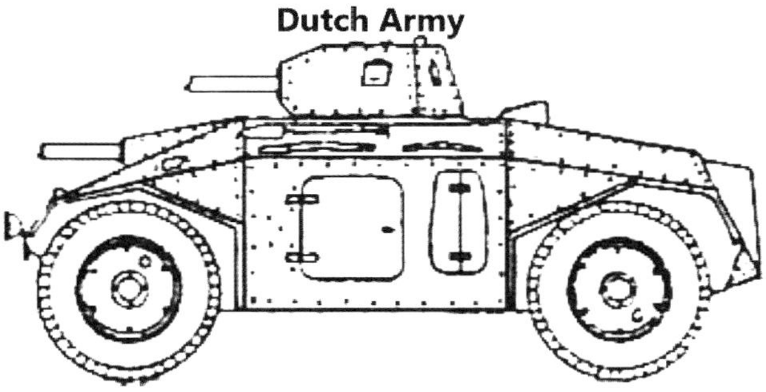

40M Csaba command/signal armoured car

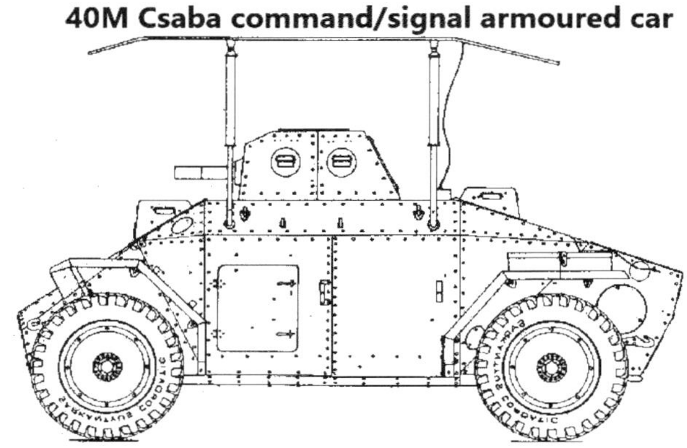

Armoured cars designed or based on Nicholas Straussler designs. (Bajtos Iván)

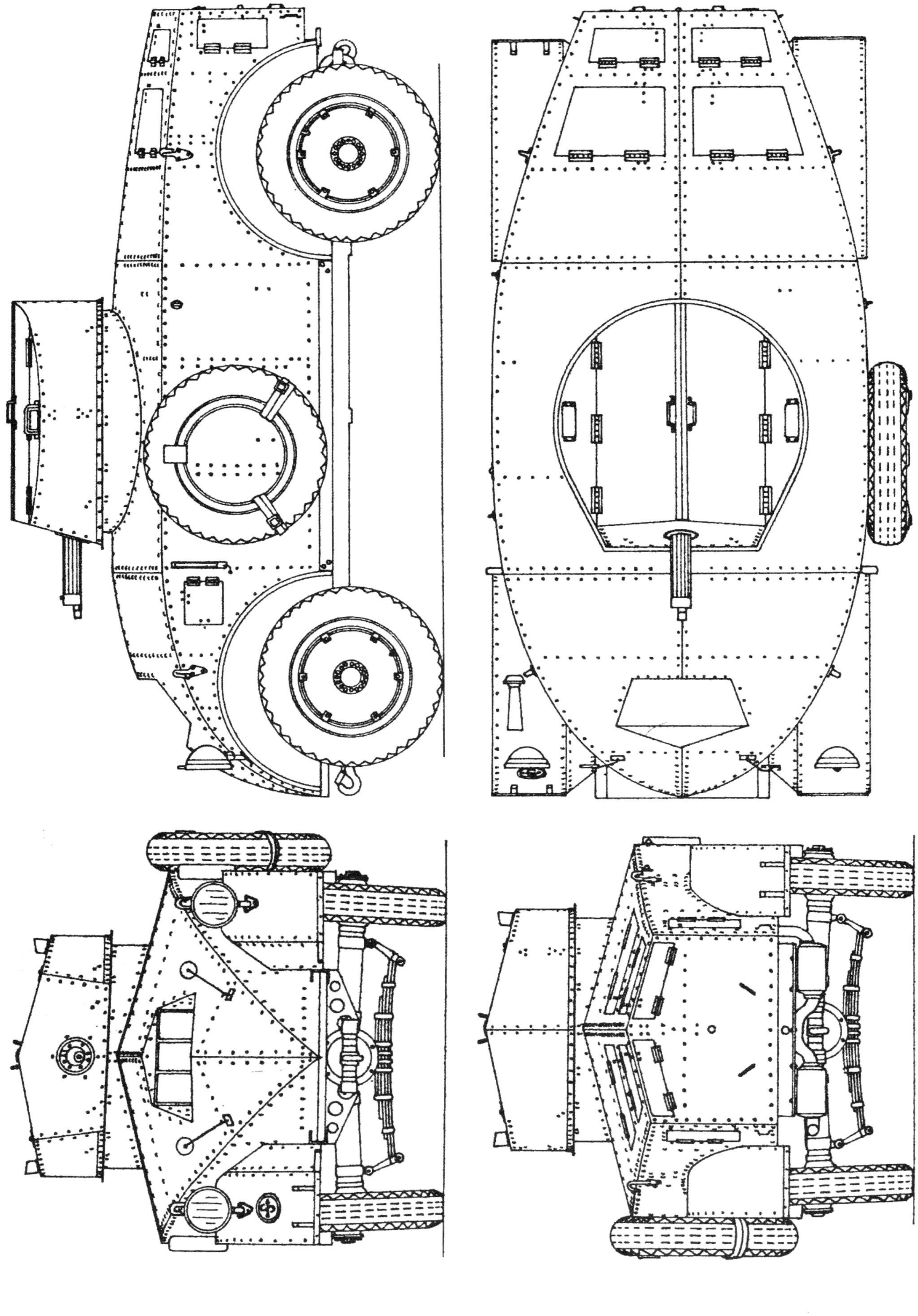

A.C.2 armoured car with Alvis Ltd. made hull and turret with Vickers machine gun. (Bajtos Iván)

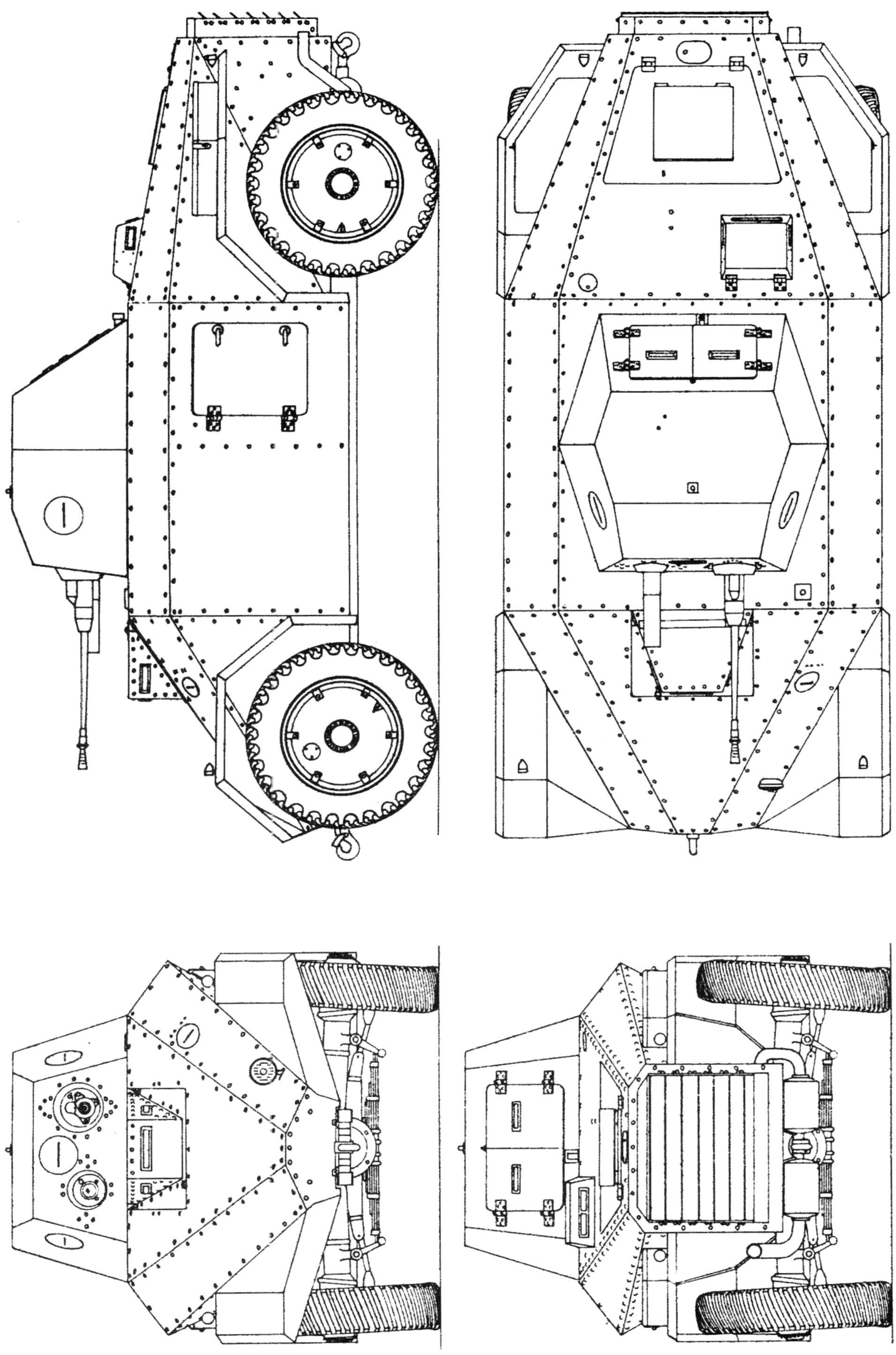

A.C.2 armoured car with Hungarian made hull and turret. (Bajtos Iván)

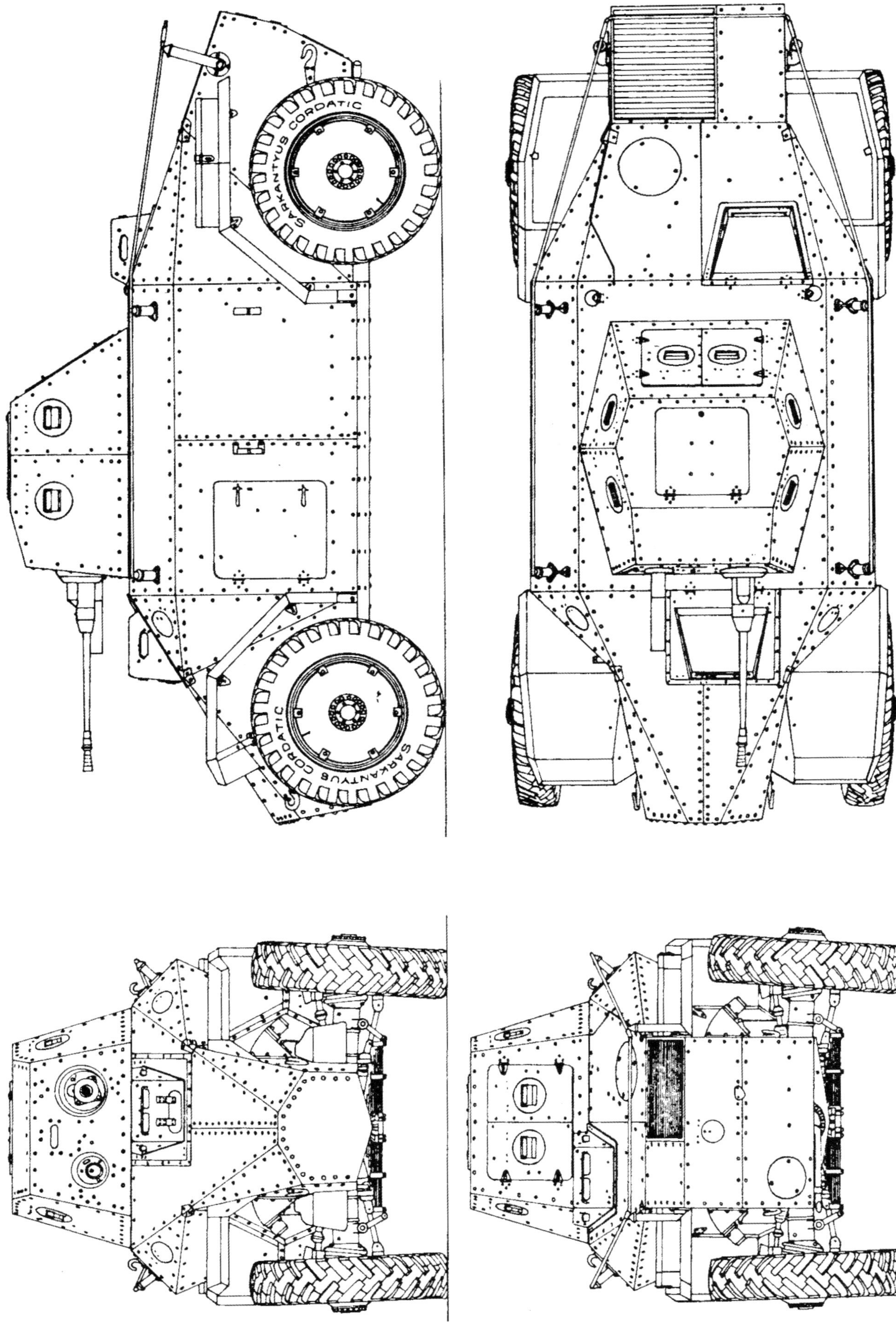

39 M. Csaba armoured car (Bajtos Iván)

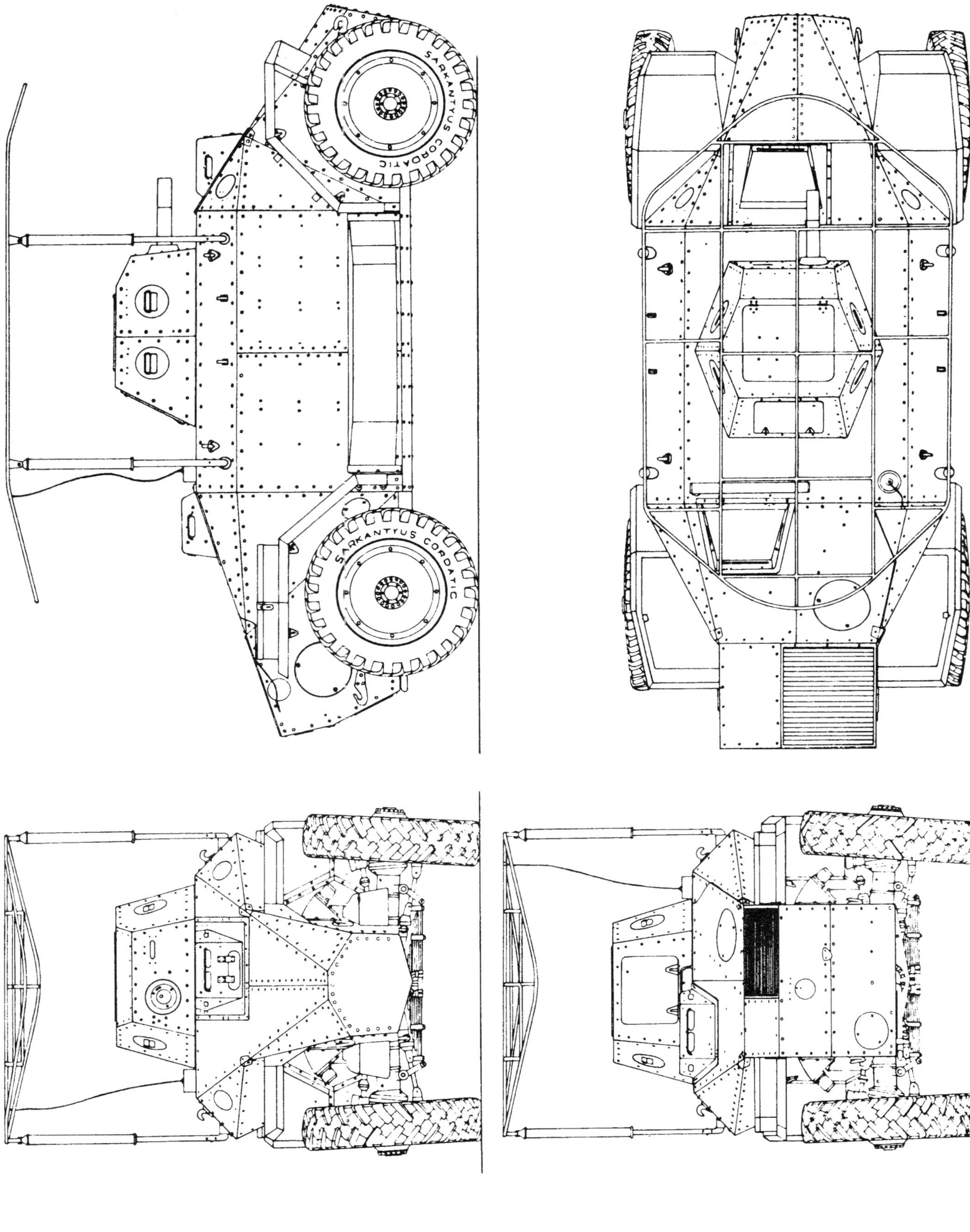

40 M. Csaba command/signal armoured car. (Bajtos Iván)

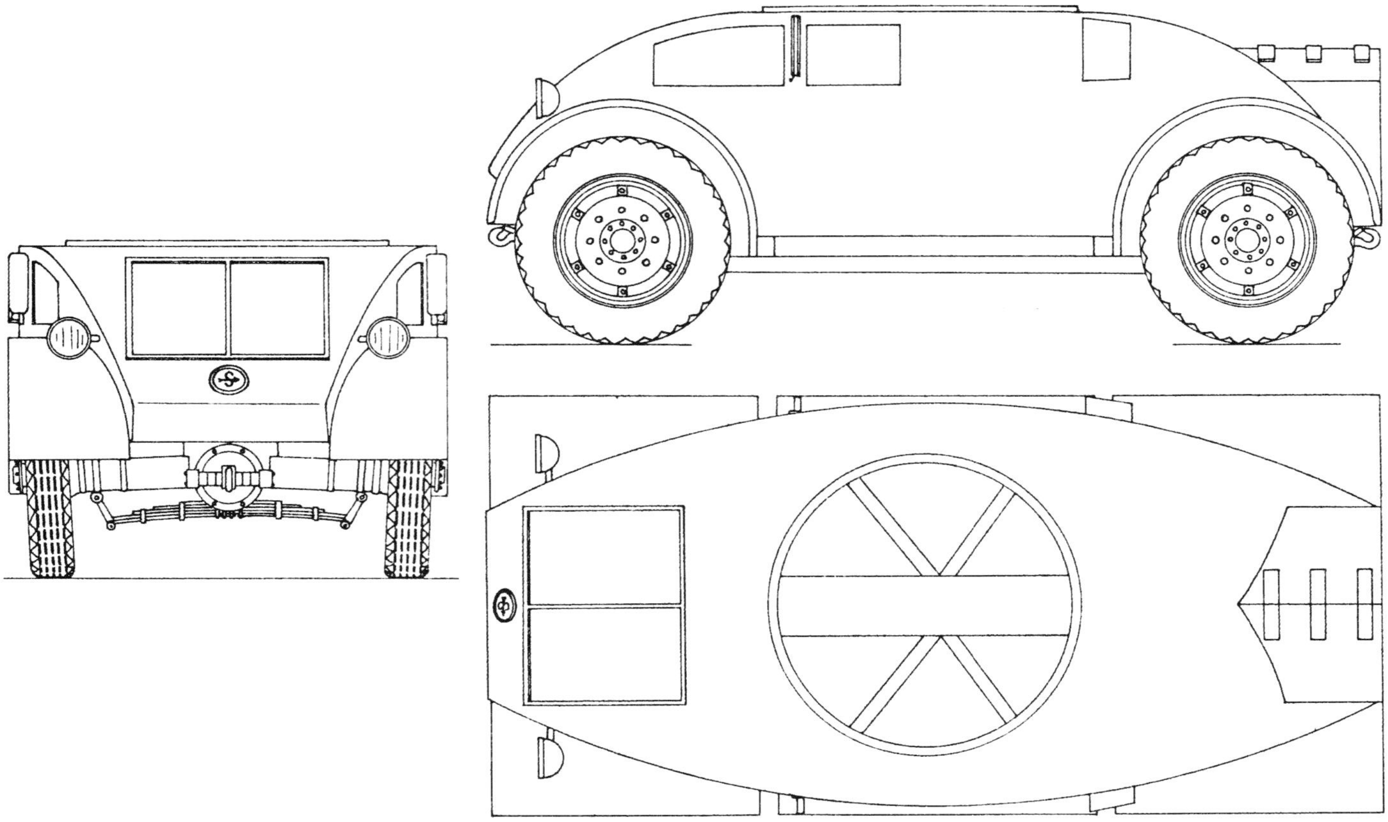

A.C.1 armoured car with a wooden superstructure made by Weiss Manfred Factory. (Bajtos Iván)

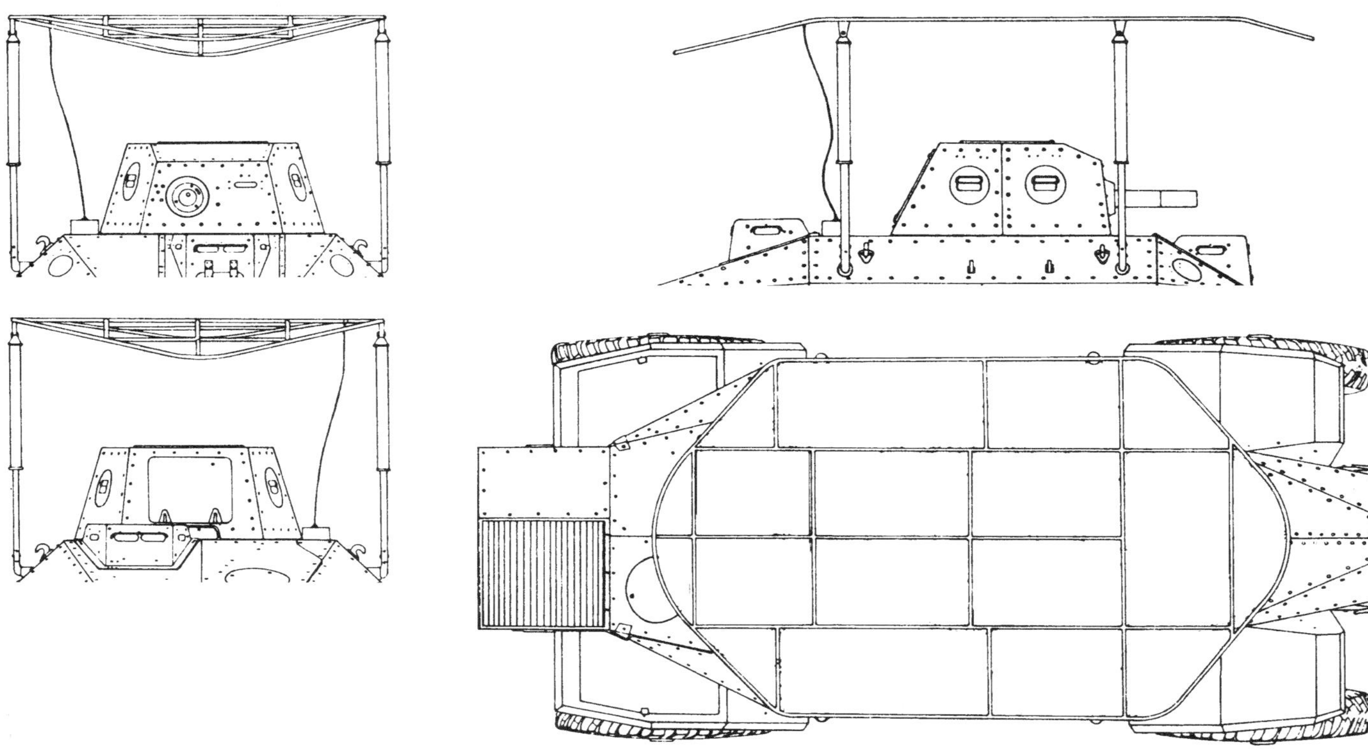

The frame antenna system of the 40 M. Csaba command/signal armoured car. (Bajtos Iván)

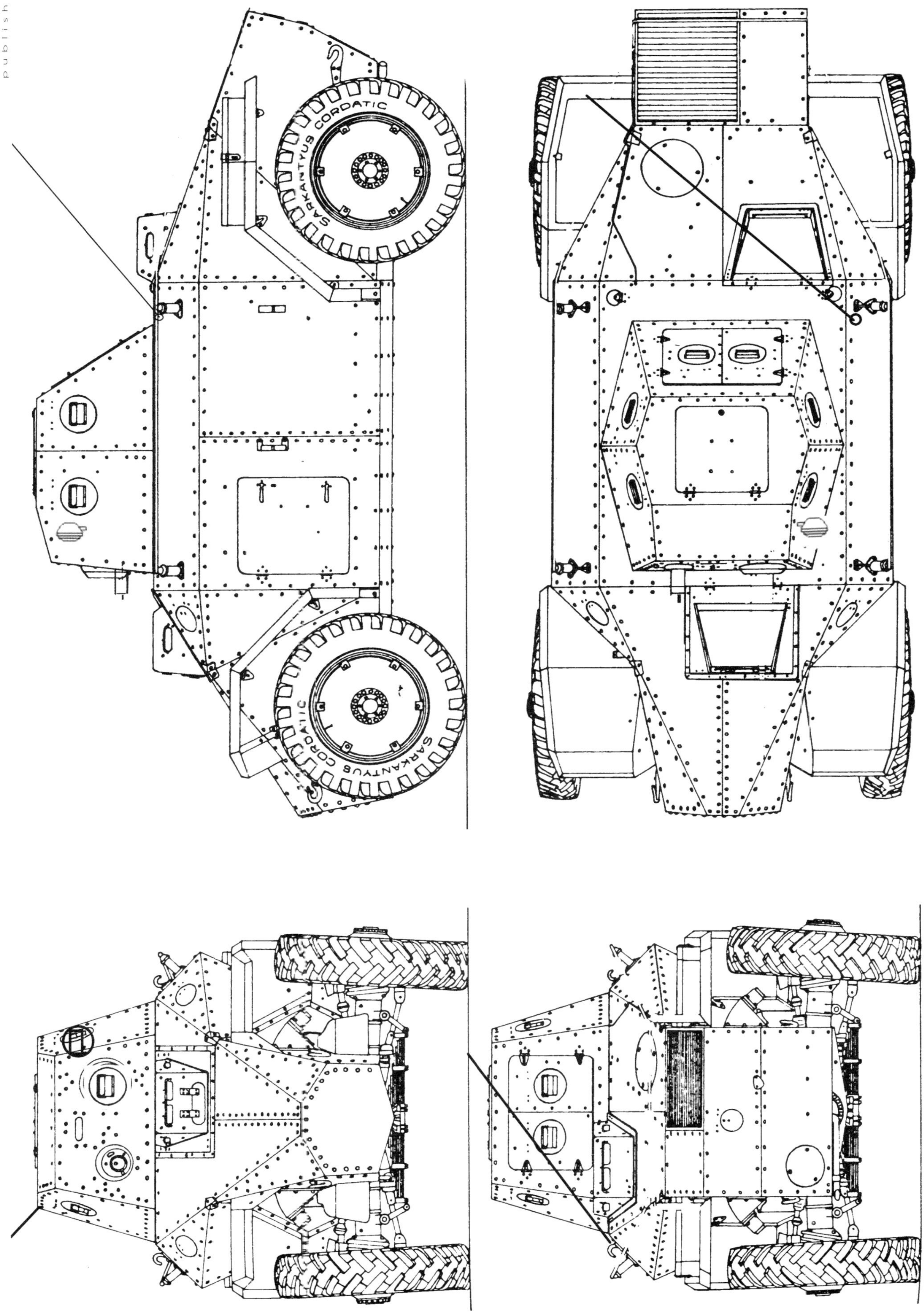

Police version of the 39 M. Csaba armoured car.(based on Bajtos Iván)

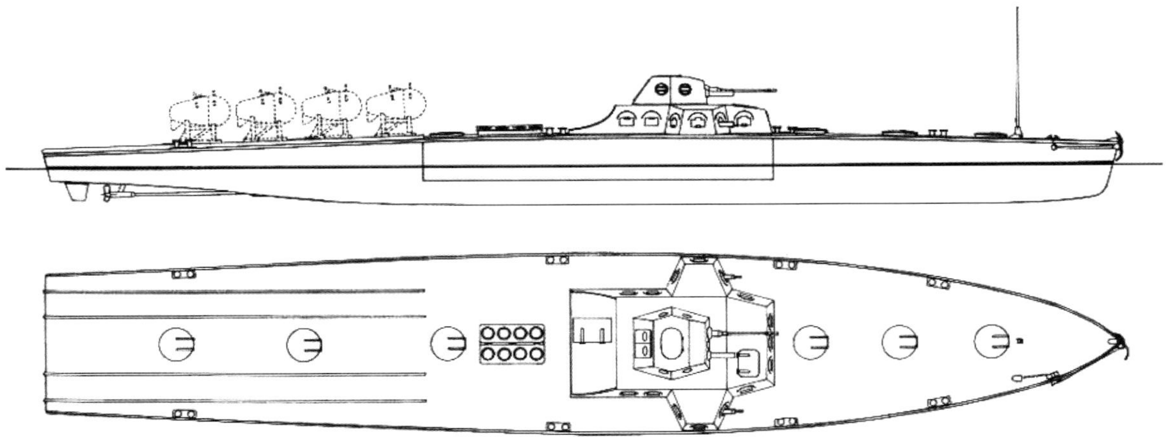

PAM Armoured Minesweeper Boat of the Hungarian River Forces with 39 M. Csaba turret. (Benczúr László)

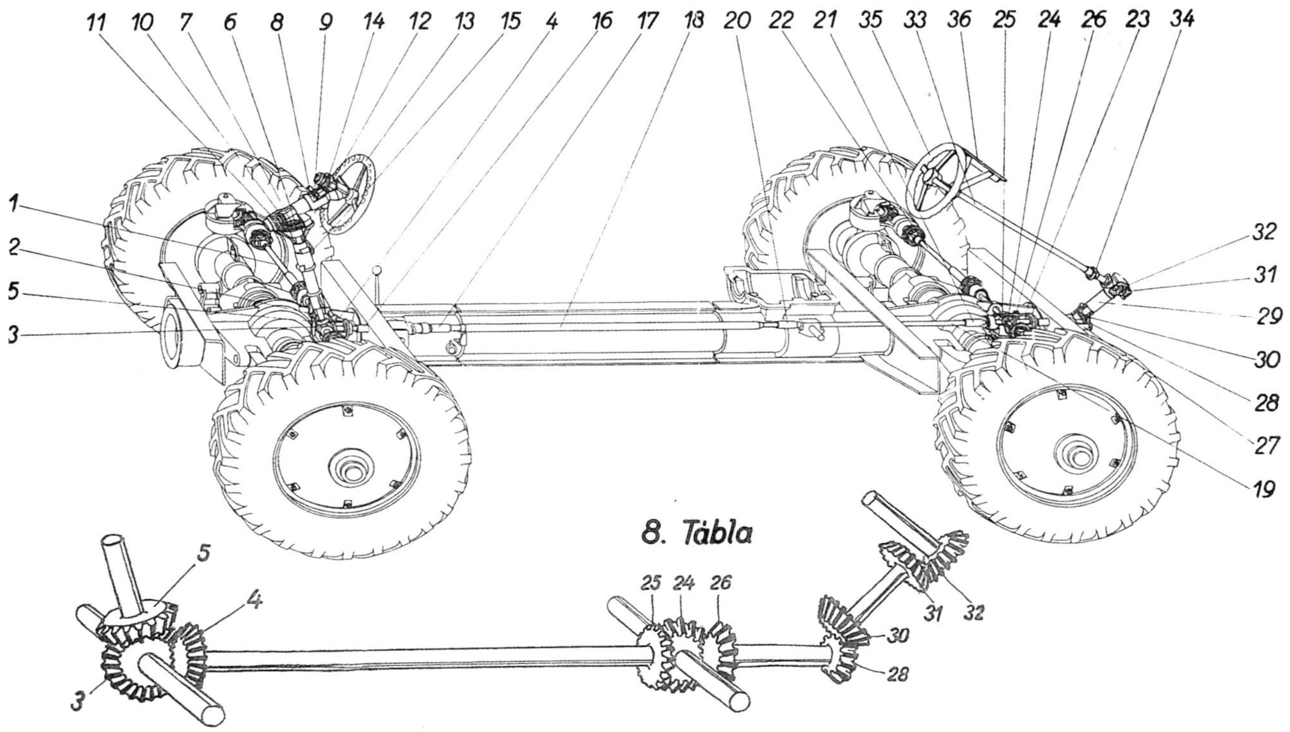

Transmission and running gear system of the Csaba armoured car with front and rear driver positions. (Service Manual)

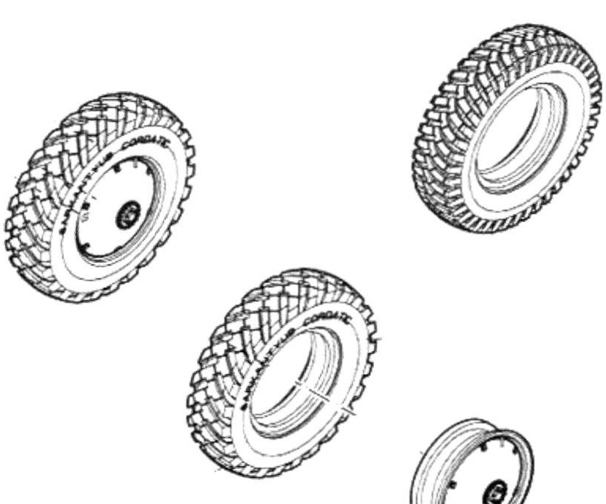

On the right is the more thickly ribbed tyer version used on the early types, on the left are the CORDATIC "spur" pattern tyers.

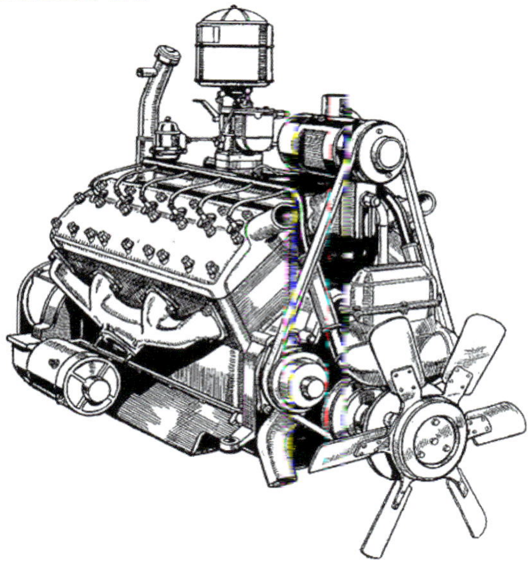

The Csaba armoured cars were powered by a 90 hp Ford V-8 truck engine, the truck ventilator system was replaced by a larger cooling system. (Service Manual)

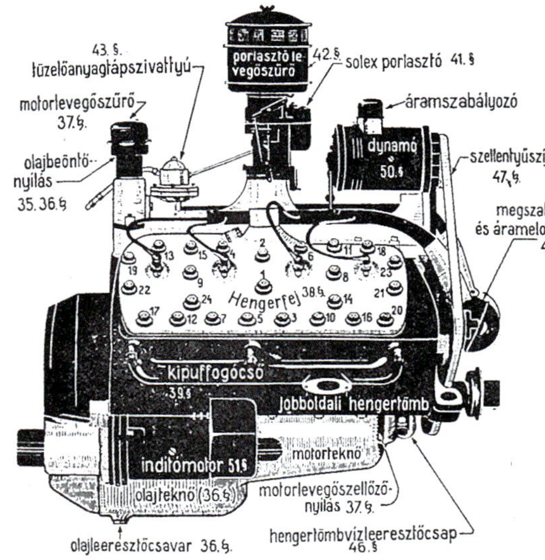

Side wiev of the 90 hp Ford V-8 engine. (Service Manual)

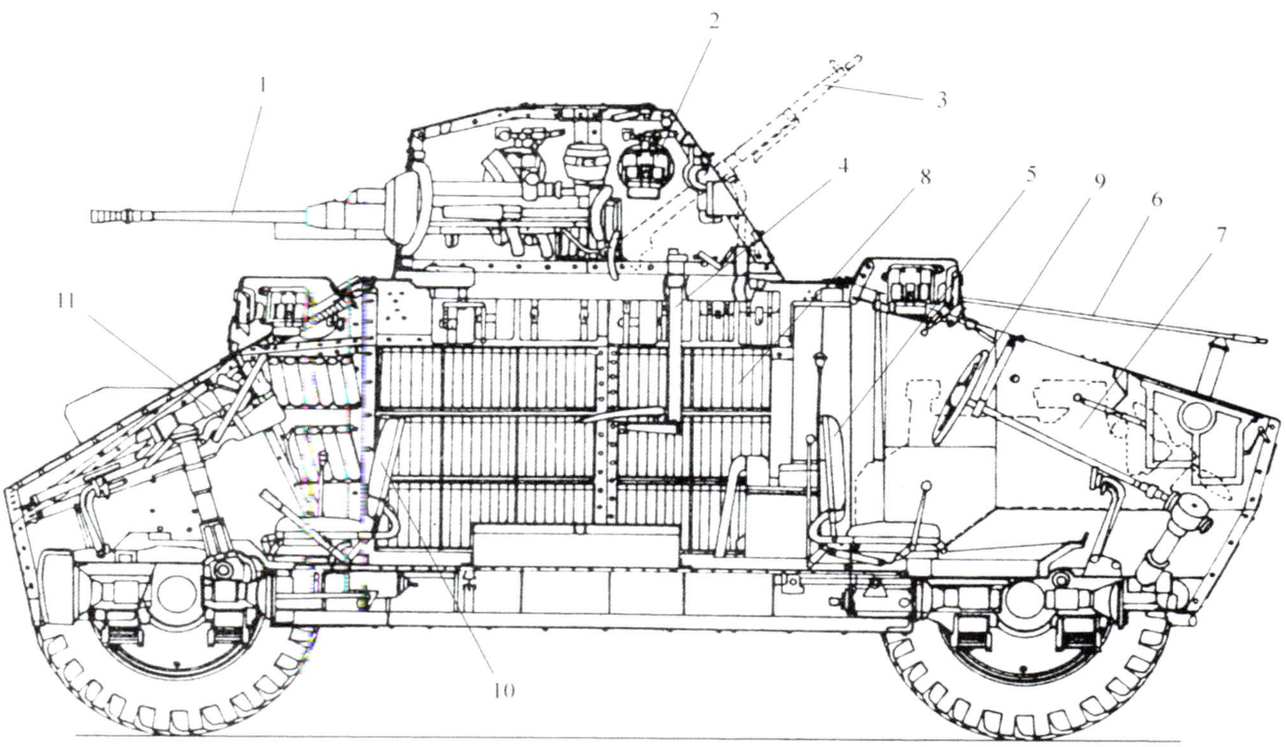

Internal layout of the 39 M. Csaba armoured car; 1.- 20mm 36 M. anti-tank rifle, 2.- observation port, 3.- 8mm 31 M. light machine gun, 4. – gunner's seat, 5.- rear driver's seat, 6.- handrail antenna, 7.- engine, 8.- ammunition boxes, 9.- rear steering wheel, 10.- front driver's seat, 11.- front steering wheel. (based on Service Manual)

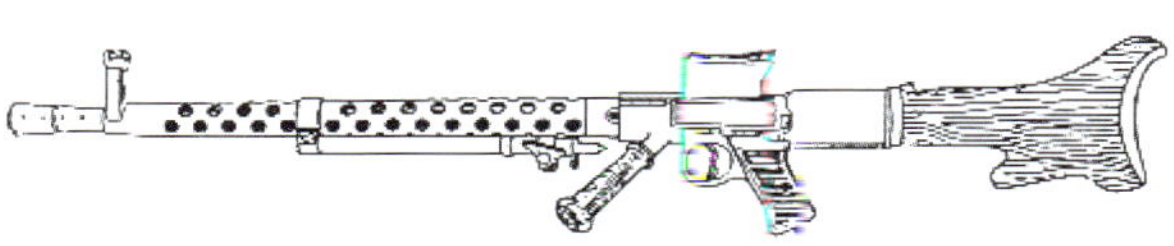

The 8mm 31 M. Solothurn light machine gun used in dual, anti-aircraft and land role on the 39 M. Csaba armoured car. (Service Manual)

The 8mm 31 M. Manlicher carbine used by the crew for self-defence. (Service Manual)

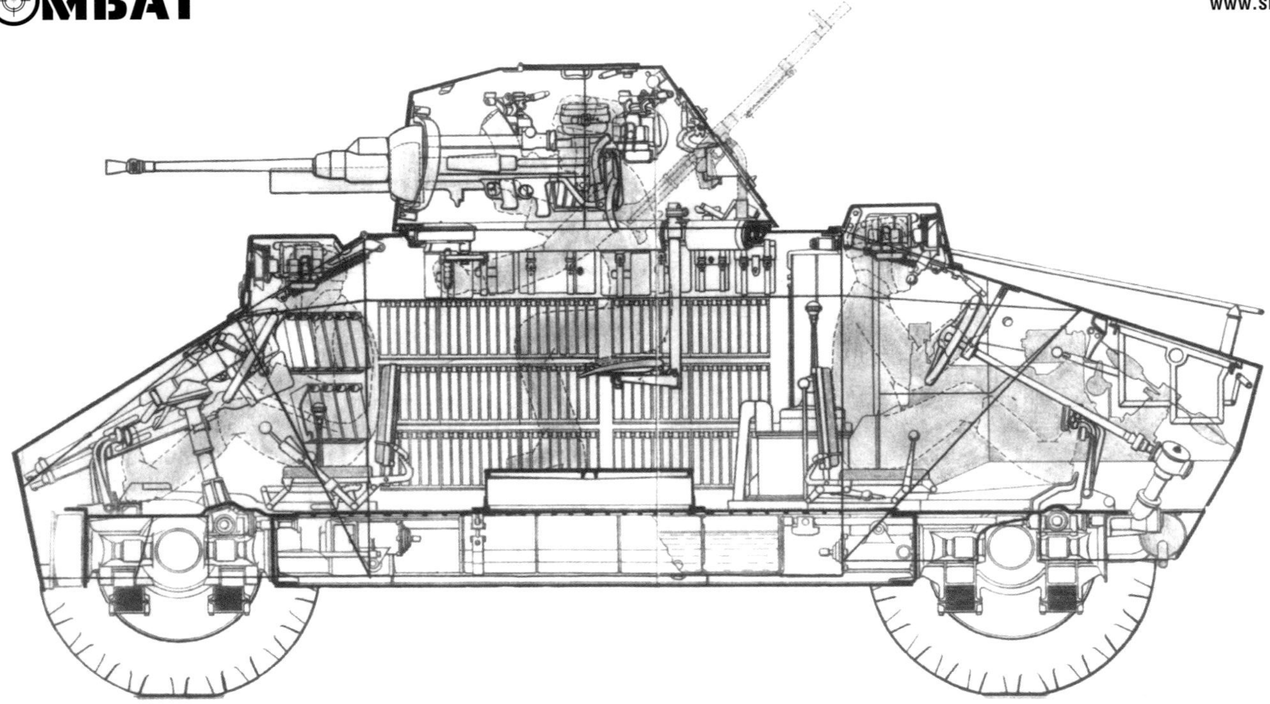

Position of the drivers and gunner in blue, machine guns in red, engine in grey. (based on Service Manual)

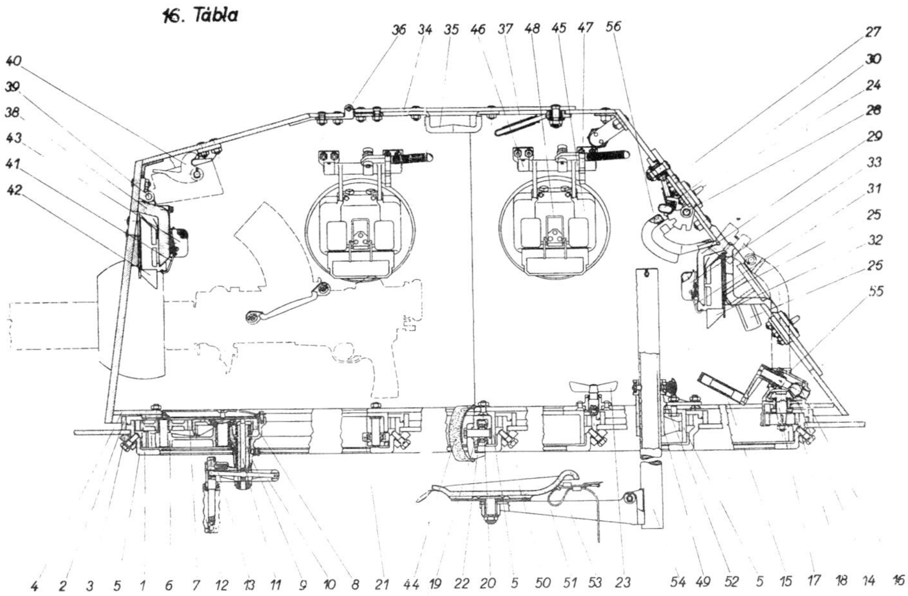

Side drawing of the turret with the observation ports and the gunner seat attached to the turret wall. (Service Manual)

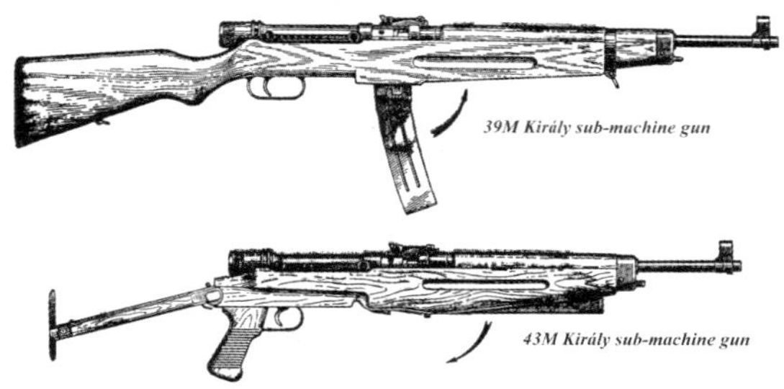

The crew of the Csaba armoured car got Hungarian 9mm 39 and 43 M. Király sub machine guns. (Service Manual)

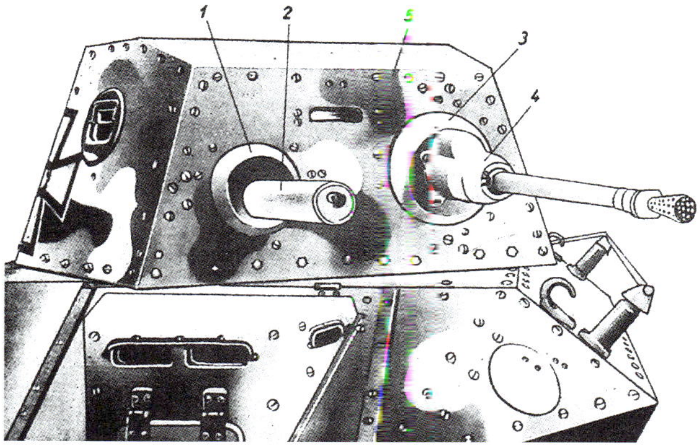

Locations on the 39 M. Csaba turret; weapon ports 1.,3., weapons; 2. machine gun and 4. anti-tank rifle and one visor slot 5. above them. (Service Manual)

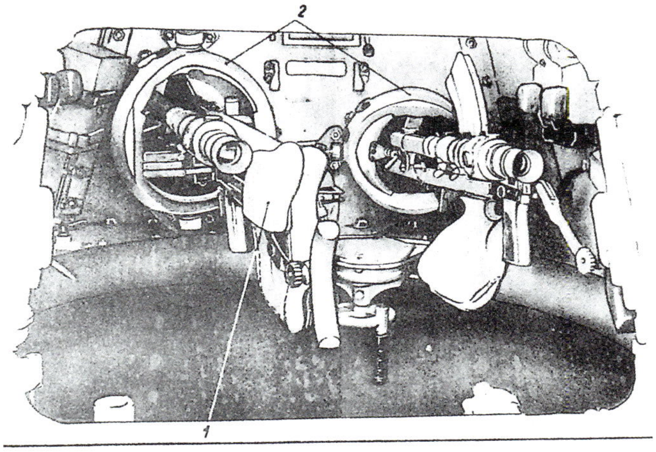

Inside drawings of the turret of 39 M. Csaba armoured car, the 2. indicate the weapon's mantels for the machine gun and the anti-tank rifle. (Service Manual)

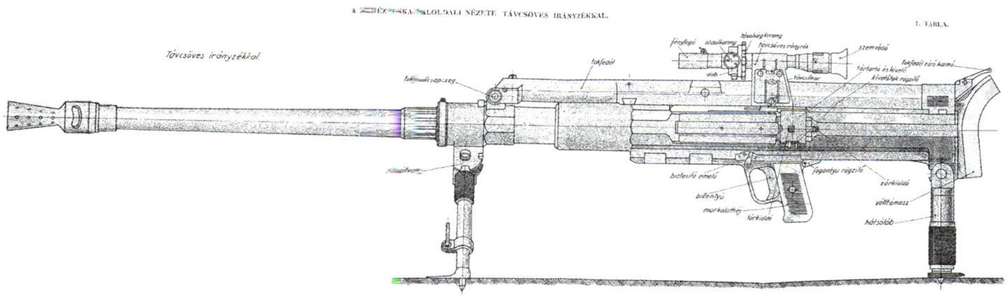

The side view of the 20mm 36 M. Solothurn anti-tank rifle with bipod and rear leg, these were removed from the weapon, when it was installed into the turret. (Service Manual)

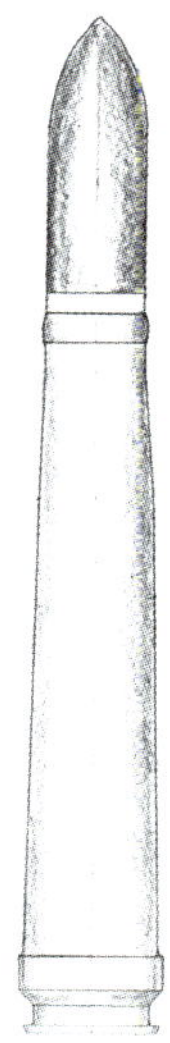

The 20mm shell of the 20mm 36 M. Solothurn anti-tank rifle. (Service Manual)

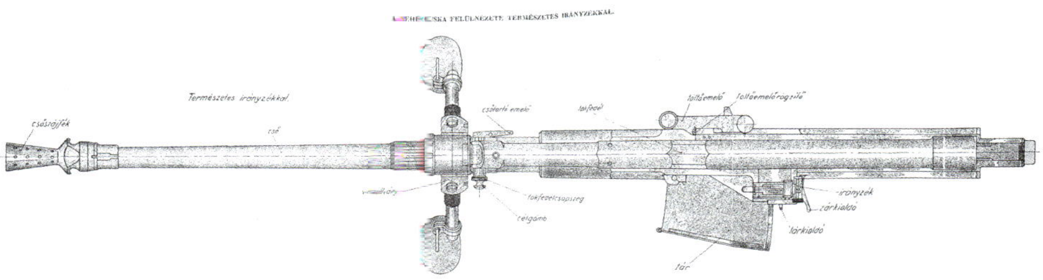

Top view of the 20mm 36 M. Solothurn anti-tank rifle. (Service Manual)

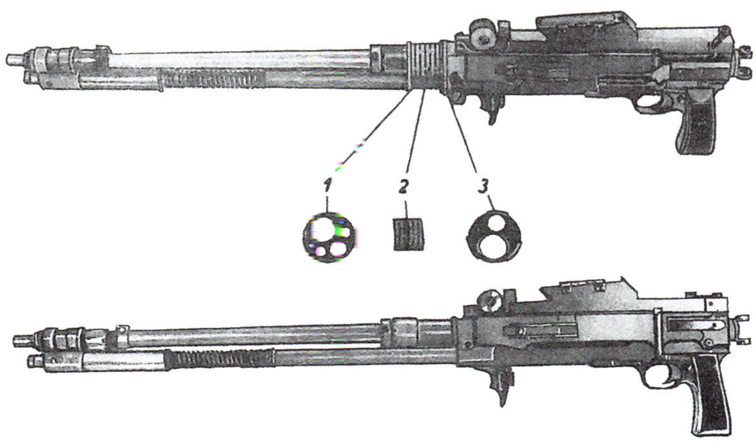

8mm 34/37 M. Gebauer machine gun. (Service Manual)

The crew also was armed with 9mm 37 M. FÉG service pistols. (Service Manual)

R/4. adókészülék.

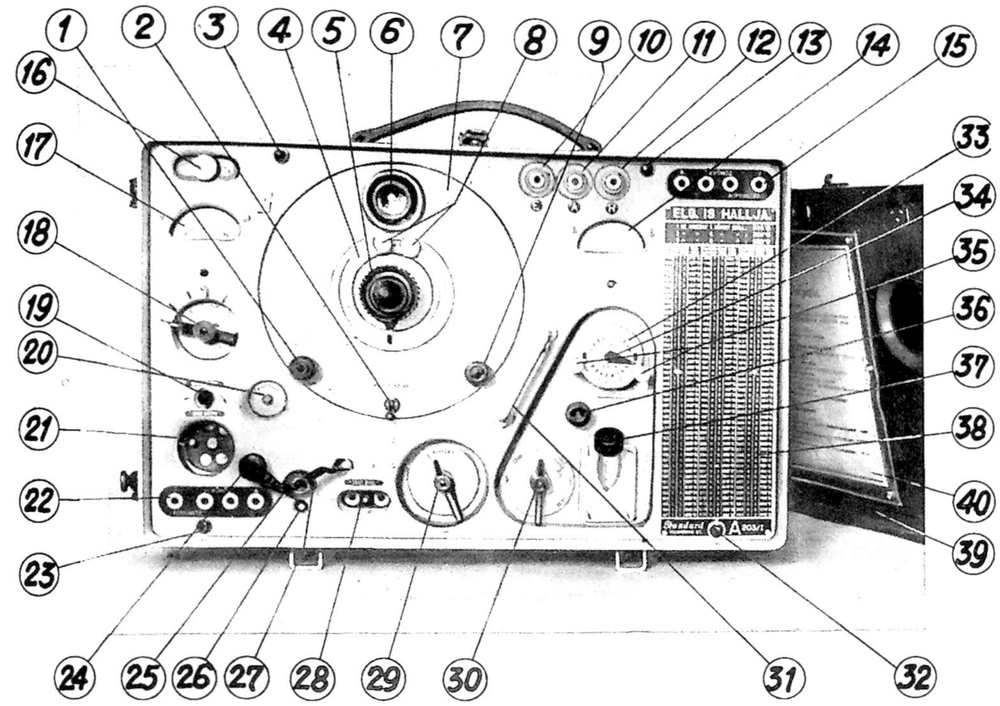

10. ábra.

1.) Hullámbeállitó rögzitő fogantyuja.

2.) Skálavilágitás ki-be kapcsoló.

3.) 13.) 23.) és 32.) Megoldandó csavarok a készüléknek a dobozból való kiszerelésekor.

4.) Körsin az ütközők számára.

5.) Hullámbeállitó durva állitó fogantyuja.

6.) Hullámbeállitó skála leolvasó ablak nagyitó üveggel.

7.) Hullámbeállitó szerkezet.

8.) A körsinen állitható ütközők.

9.) Hullámbeállitó finom állitó fogantyuja.

10.) Ellensulycsatlakozó szoritócsavar.

11.) Antennacsatlakozó szoritócsavar.

12.) Antenna-rövidítő csatlakozó szoritócsavar.

14.) Antenna-árammérő müszer.

15.) és 22.) Adó-vevő összekötő-hüvelyszerelvény.

The signal equipment of the Csaba armoured car consisted of one R/4. radio transmitter. (Signal Manual)

R/4. vevőkészülék.

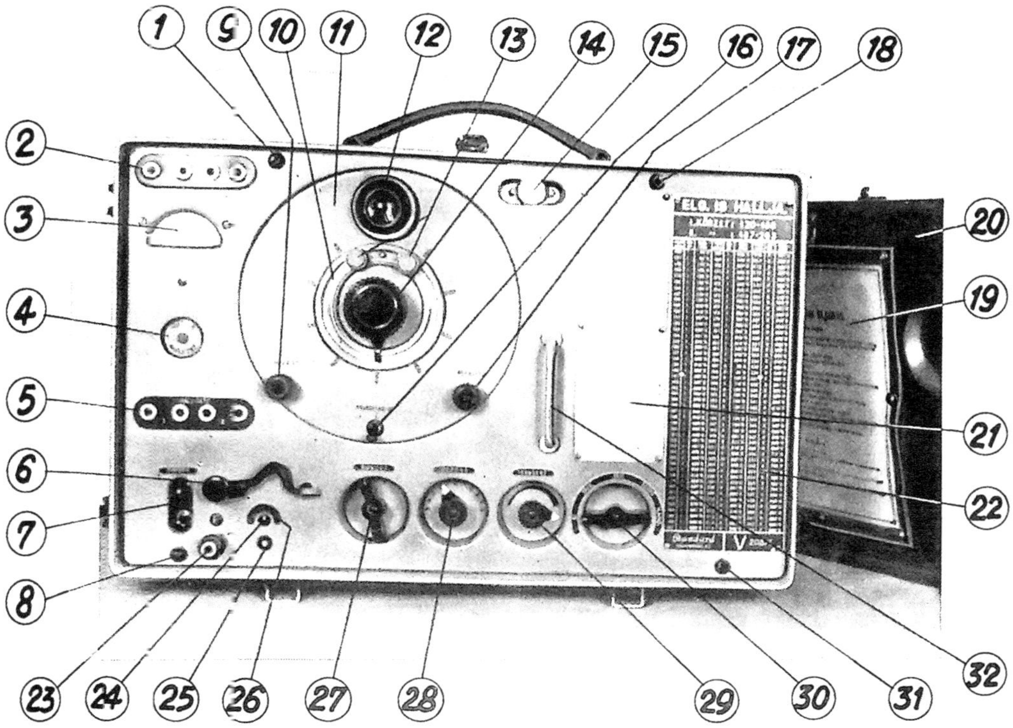

11. ábra.

1.) 8.) 18.) és 31.) Megoldandó csavarok a készüléknek a dobozból való kisszereléséhez.

2.) Adó-vevő összekötő hüvelyszerelvény.

3.) Ellenőrzőműszer.

4.) Átkapcsoló nyomógomb az ellenőrzőműszerhez.

5.) Fejhallgató csatlakozó hüvelyszerelvény.

6.) Bőrszíjon lógó fogantyú vevő utánállitáshoz.

7.) Akkumulátor-vevő összekötőkábel csatlakozó dugasz-szerelvény.

9.) Hullámbeállitó rögzitő fogantyuja.

10.) Körsin az ütközők állitásához.

11.) Hullámbeállitó szerkezet.

12.) Hullámbeállitó skála leolvasó ablak nagyitó üveggel.

13.) Körsinen állitható ütközők.

14.) Hullámbeállitó durva állitó fogantyúja.

15.) Szerelvénylap-megvilágitó lámpa. ./.

The signa equipment of the Csaba armoured car consisted of one R/4. radio reciver. (Signal Manual)

Az R/4. rádiókészülékek elhelyezése a pc.gk-kban.

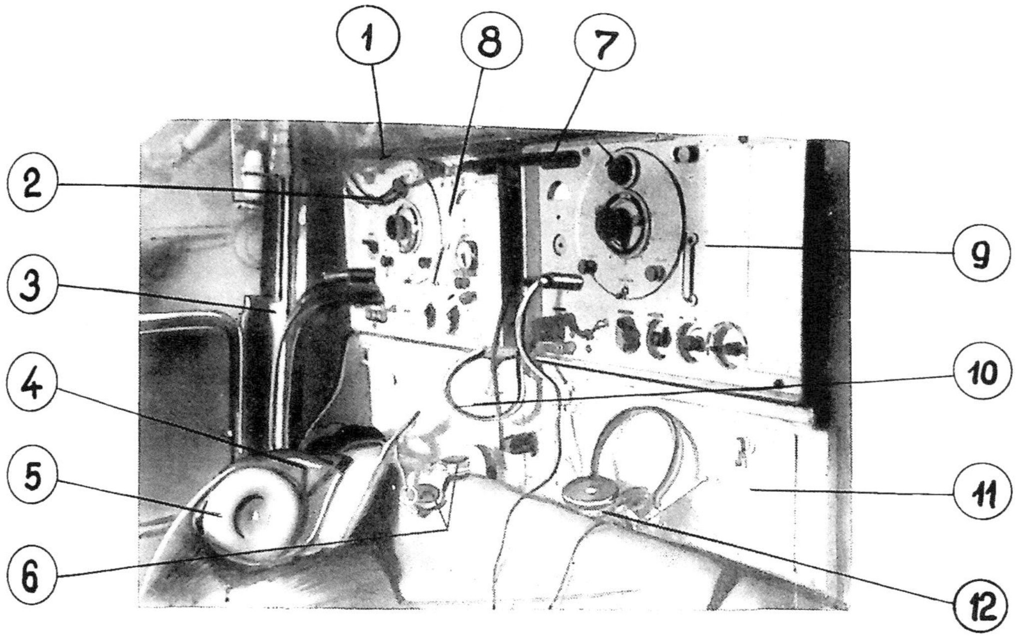

33. ábra.

1.) Antenna-bevezető.
2.) Ellensúly-bevezető.
3.) Botantenna.
4.) Bukósisak.
5.) Gumipárnás fejhallgató a bukósisakba szerelve.
6.) Gégemikrofon.
7.) Adó-vevő összekötőkábel.
8.) Adókészülék.
9.) Vevőkészülék.
10.) Tartozék-szekrény baloldali rész.
11.) Tartozék-szekrény jobboldali rész.
12.) Külön (be nem épitett) fejhallgató.

The installation of the R/4. radio reciver and transmitter in the armoured car. (Signal Manual)

A Csaba pc.gk. rádió-akkumulátor telepei a pc.gk. akkumulátor-szekrényében elhelyezve.

37. ábra.

1.) Akkumulátor-szekrény.
2.) A felső akkumulátor + sarka (az egész akkumulátortelep – 12 V-os sarka).
3.) Az alsó akkumulátor-sarka (egyúttal az egész akkumulátor-telep - sarka).
4.) A – sarok testelő kábele.
5.) A felső akkumulátor – sarka.
6.) Alsó és felső akkumulátor sorbakötő kábel.
7.) Felső 6 V-os akkumulátor.
8.) Alsó 6 V-os akkumulátor.
9.) Az alsó akkumulátor + sarka.

The Bosch battery was situated in the back of the armoured car. (Signal Manual)

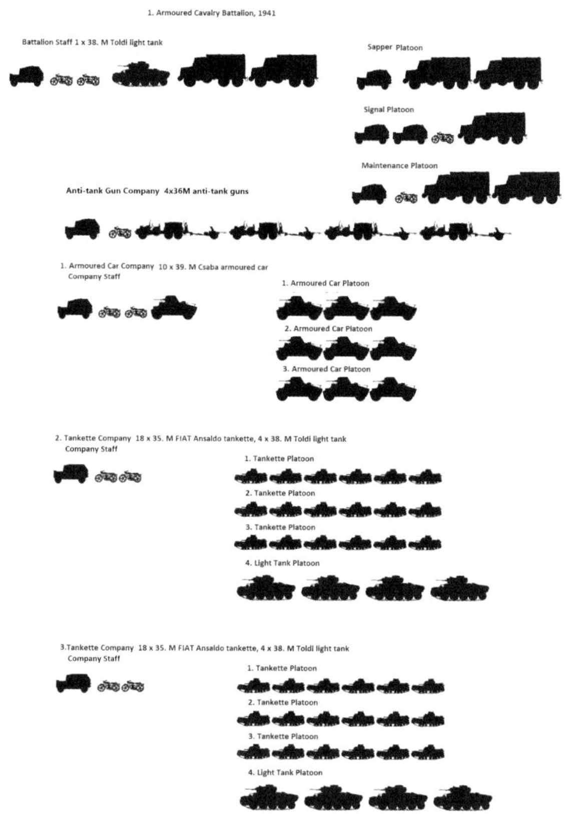

OB 1941 1st and 2nd Armoured Cavalry Battalions

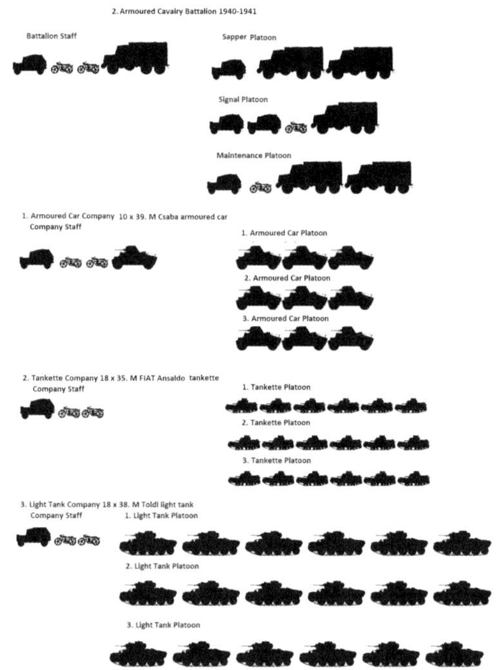

OB 1940-1941 1st and 2nd Armoured Cavalry Battalions.

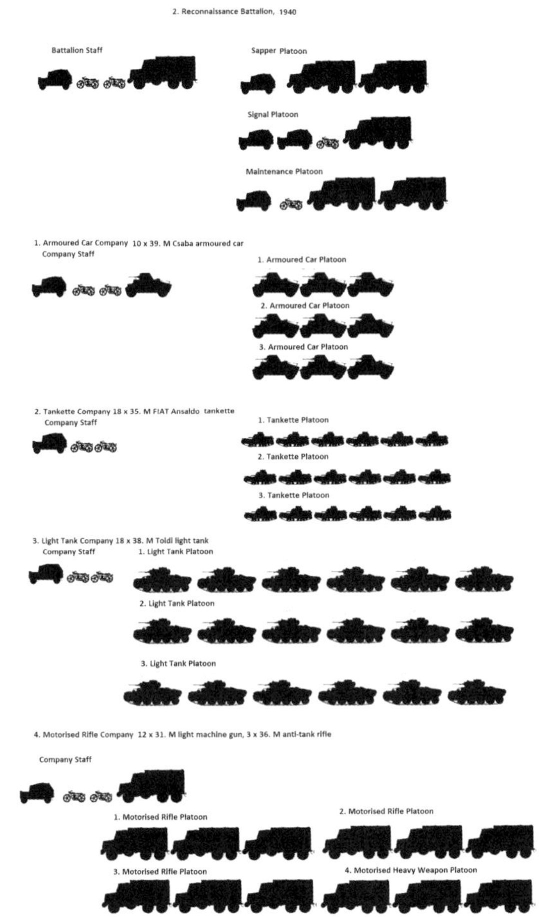

OB 1940, 1st and 2nd Reconnaissance Battalions.

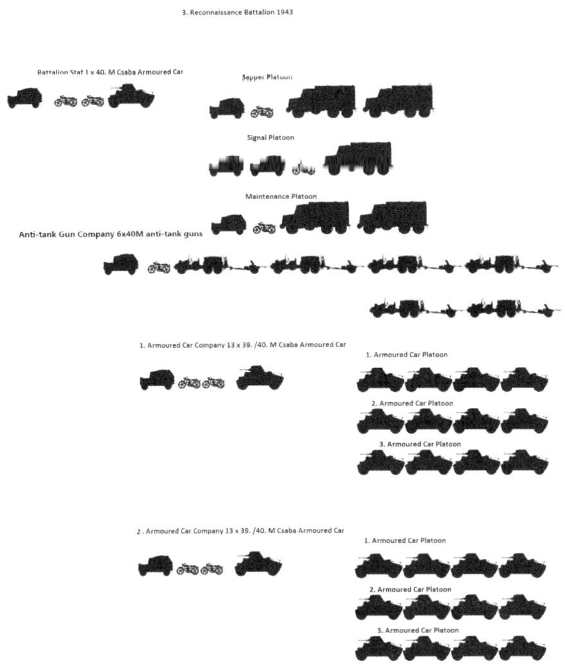

OB 1943 3rd Reconnaissance Battalion

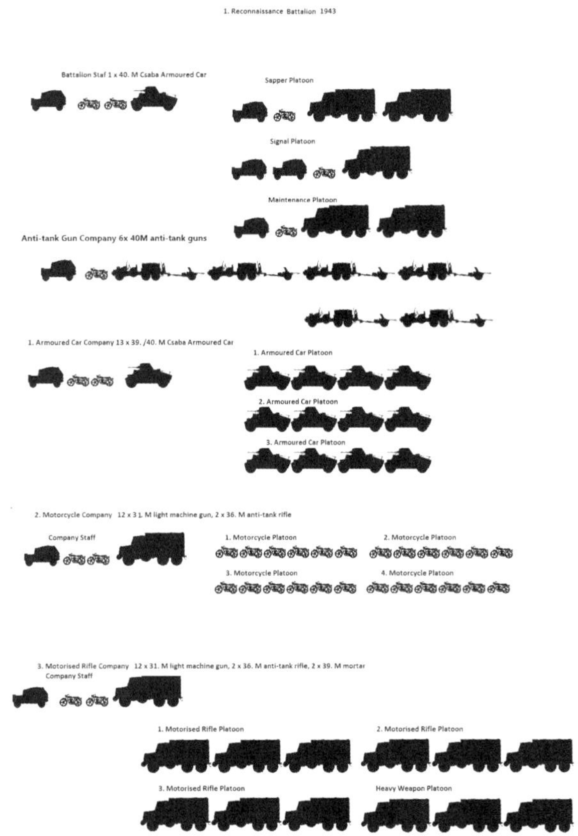

OB 1943 1st and 2nd Reconnaissance Battalions

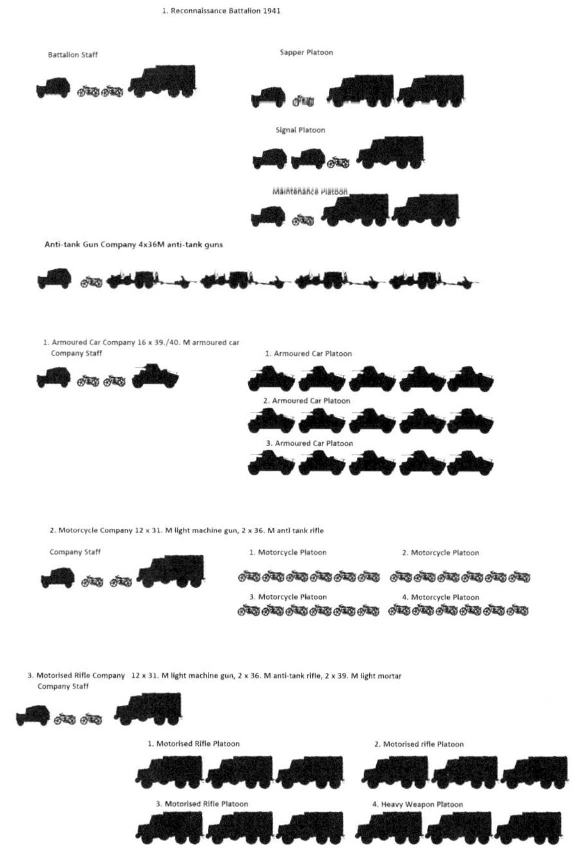

OB 1941 1st and 2nd Reconnaissance Battalions

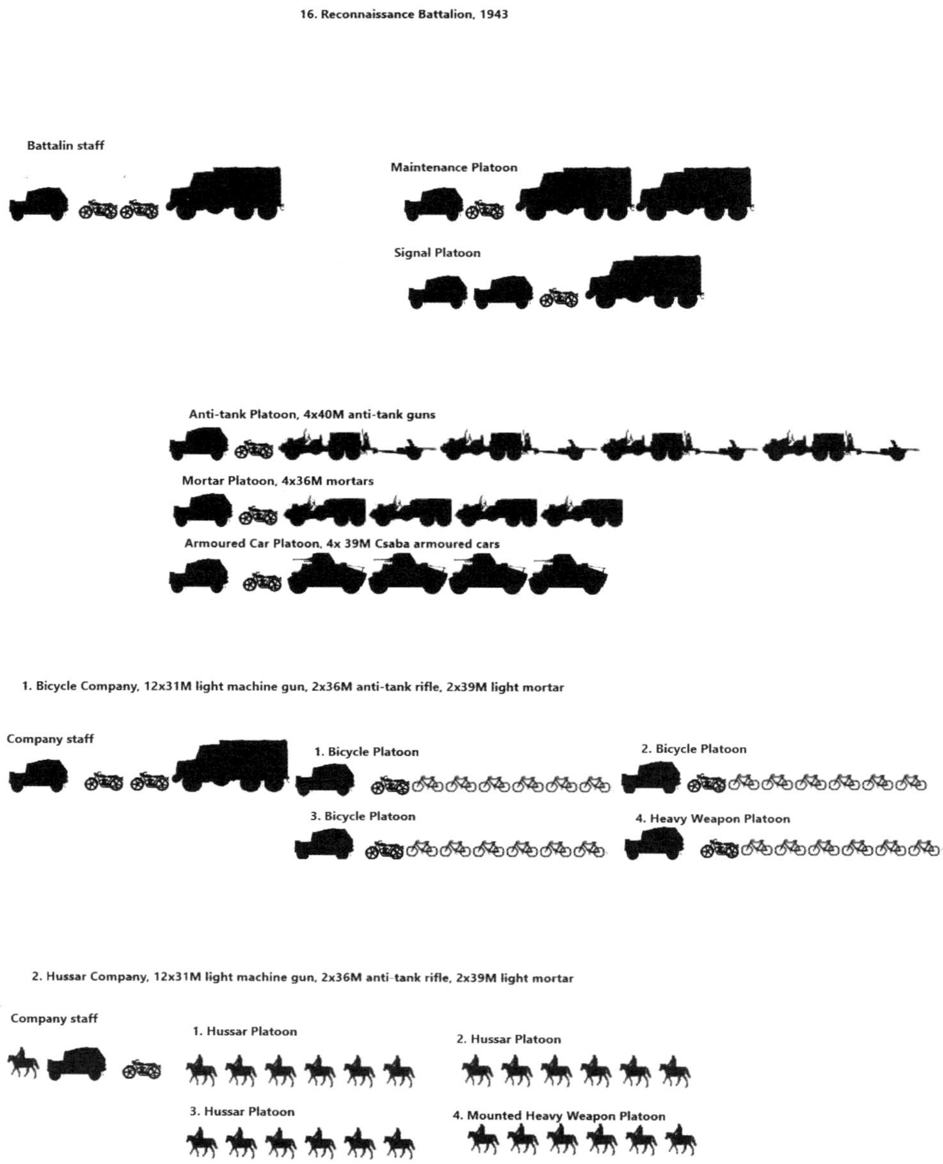

OB 1943 reconnaissance battalions of the first line infantry divisions.

The unserviceable armoured cars were collected and prepared for rail transportation back to Hungary by the end of the operation in Ukraine in November-December 1941. The armoured cars were protected with canvas cover, on the left is a 40 M. command car with frame antenna. (Fortepan/Korbuly)

The armoured and wheeled vehicles of the armoured car company of the 1st Armoured Cavalry Battalion returning from Ukraine. The second armoured car is the Pc.139. (Mujzer collection)

Armoured troopers posing in front of their 39 M. Csaba armoured car, dressed in mechanic overalls and field blouse and trouser, one of them armed with 9mm MP-40 submachine gun. (Mujzer collection)

Advancing 39 M. Csaba armoured car drove through a destroyed village at the River Don in the summer of 1942, the commander sat on the top of the turret, a good observation point but making him an easy target. (Móker József)

Motorbicycle platoon and 39 M. Csaba armoured car of the 1st Reconnaissance Battalion advancing towards the River Don. The battalion unit sign, a white lightning bolt painted into a white rhombus which was the unit sign of the 1st Armoured Field Division. (War Correspondent Company)

Heavily camouflaged 39 M. Csaba armoured cars and resting crew wearing mechanic overalls, and visor hats at the River Don in summer 1942. (Mujzer collection)

During the winter of 1942-1943, the 1st Reconnaissance Battalion as its Division was in reserve. The armoured vehicles got whitewashed winter camouflage. Crew posing on the 39 M. Csaba armoured car next to a ruined orthodox church. (Virág Ajtony)

March 1943, the remains of the 1st Armoured Field Division took part in the farewell ceremony at the football stadium in Kiev, before returning home after the winter battles. On the left corner, one 39 M. Csaba armoured car is visible. (Fortepan)

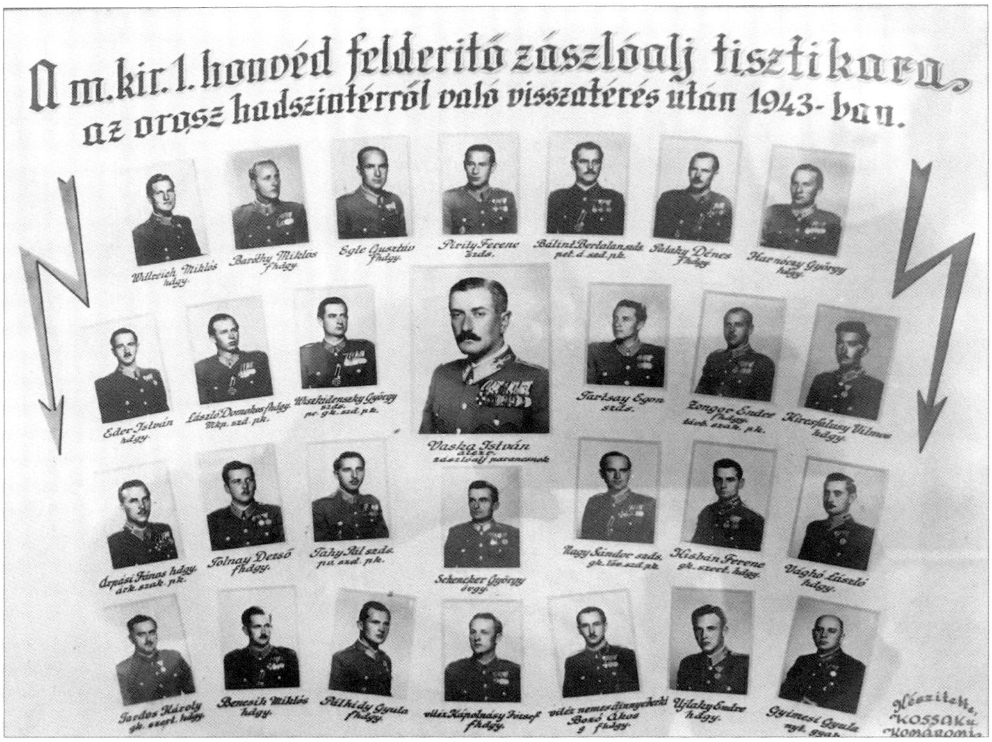

Professional officers of the 1st Reconnaissance Battalion in 1943, led by Lieutenant Colonel István Vaska, numbered 28 officers, organised into 5 companies, officially the 1st Armoured Train Company also belonged to the battalion. (Virág Ajtony)

39 M. Csaba armoured car belonged to the 102nd Independent Armoured Company of the Hungarian Occupation Forces in 1943-1944. (Karai Sándor)

On 17 April 1944 the troopers of the 2nd Reconnaissance Battalion watching the artillery preparation before the attack at Nadworna, Galicia. The armoured cars had three-digit tactical numbers started with 13, probably belonged to the 3rd Armoured Car Platoon/ Armoured Car Company. The armoured cars were painted in three-tone camouflage. (ECPA)

Hungarian mountain troops wearing the distinctive visor hat field cap posing around a 39 M. Csaba armoured car belongs to the 2nd Reconnaissance Battalion. The armoured troopers on the right and the centre wearing their new 43 M. smoke grey, German-style two pieces armoured uniform. (Fortepan)

A bridge collapsed under famous sand yellow coloured 39 M. Csaba armoured car during the advance around Nadworna in April 1944. The tactical number, 124 indicates, this vehicle belonged to the 2nd Platoon of the Armoured Car company. The white eagle was the battalion sign; the white triangle was the unit sign of the 2nd Armoured Division. (ECPA)

Advancing command group of the 2nd Reconnaissance Battalion in Galicia with 40 M. Csaba command/signal armoured car Pc.408, surrounded by dispatch riders on Puch G350 motorbikes following Skoda and Mercedes staff cars. The Hungarians wearing whitewashed 35M steel helmets. (ECPA)

Another disabled 39 M. Csaba armoured car, tactical number 133, belonged to the 3rd Platoon, painted to sand yellow colour. Soldiers trying to push the armoured car out of the muddy grass field in Galicia. (ECPA)

Sand yellow coloured 39 M. Csaba armoured cars of the 2nd Reconnaissance Battalion, the battalion and divisional unit signs painted on the frontal armour plate of the armoured cars. The armoured crew and Hungarian cavalry troops waiting for the marching order at the slope of the Carpathian Mountain in April 1944. (ECPA)

The 3rd Reconnaissance Battalion belonged to the 1st Cavalry Division, having two armoured companies equipped with 39 M. and 40 M. Csaba armoured cars. The vehicles were painted dark olive-green and wearing the white cross black square military insignia. (Fortepan/Lissák)

Soviet soldiers examining an abandoned Hungarian 39 M. Csaba armoured car in the Carpathian Mountain during the Soviet summer offensive in 1944. (Mujzer collection)

Armoured reconnaissance troopers and officers posing in front of their 39 M. Csaba armoured car, painted dark olive-green and wearing the white cross black square military insignia. (Mujzer collection)

Reserve ensigns posing on a 39 M. Csaba armoured car, armed with 42 M. Vécsey had grenades taking part of retraining program at Esztergomtábor, mobilised to screen the Hungarian-Romanian border after 23 August 1944. (Szollár János)

39 M. Csaba armoured car, Pc.152 and its crew deployed next to a Hungarian rocket launcher battery equipped with 150mm six barrelled 43 M. rocket launchers, to support the Hungarian attack at Arad in mid-September 1944. (Mujzer collection)

39 M. Csaba armoured cars belonged to the State Police Mobile Reserve lined up at the Vajdahunyad Castle in Budapest in late 1944. The armoured cars were escorted by police side-car motorcycles and cars. (Pálinkás Zsolt)

The weapons of the 39 M. Csaba armoured cars changed, the anti-tank rifles removed from the turret, only armed with one machine gun and a searchlight was added. The known number plates are RR.511 and 512. (Pálinkás Zsolt)

Movie footage of the field exercise of the Police armoured cars. The bright dark blue paint is well visible. The rail antenna was also removed from the cars, equipped only with a stick antenna. (Pálinkás Zsolt)

Right after the end of the siege of Budapest, abandoned German and Hungarian artillery pieces, on the right corner is a 39 M. Csaba armoured car with one colour camouflage. (Fortepan)

War Booty Exhibition in Moscow held in summer of 1945 alongside River Neva, on the left are captured Axis armoured cars, second from left is a 39 M. Csaba armoured car, the winter camouflage suggests, that the Hungarian armoured car was captured in Galicia, spring of 1944. (Mujzer collection)

The 1st Reconnaissance Battalion was commanded by Lieutenant Colonel Jenő Altorjay and later Lieutenant Colonel Zoltán Baló. The 2nd Reconnaissance Battalion was led by Lieutenant Colonel Endre Zádor and later Lieutenant Colonel Zoltán Török. Colonel Ferenc Révhegyi commanded the 1st Armoured Cavalry Battalion during the operation in Ukraine, on 21 August Lieutenant Colonel László Bercsényi taken over the command of the depleted 1st Armoured Cavalry Battalion.

The forward echelon of a motorized brigade consisted of the reconnaissance battalion, which was reinforced by light tank, anti-aircraft, engineer, anti-tank, machine-gun and traffic-control platoons, one light-howitzer battery and one motorized rifle company.

The reconnaissance battalions organised different platoon and company size composite units from their subordinated companies to collect information and explore the enemy locations and intentions.

The platoon size reconnaissance patrols consisted of one-two 39 M. Csaba armoured cars, one-two motorised rifle/ motorcycle/ machine gun/ anti-tank gun/sapper squads.

The company size reconnaissance team consisted of half-platoon –platoon size armoured car/ motorised rifle/ motorcycle/ machine gun/ anti-tank gun/sapper teams.

The company size reconnaissance teams deployed towards the main directions, the reconnaissance patrols deployed as flanking forces.

In early July 1941, around Zaleschyki the reconnaissance and motorised rifles of the 2nd Motorised Brigade lost two officers and 25 men killed in action, 60 men wounded in action. One-one 39 M. Csaba armoured car and 36M anti-tank gun were lost.

The difficult terrain and the operations caused significant losses to the armoured car companies, as of 01 August 8 Csaba armoured car missing from the order of battle. Although 57 39 M. Csaba armoured cars were deployed to the front, only 20 were operable in August of 1941. Another 20 unserviceable armoured cars were already sent home by rail transportation. The field repair workshops franticly worked on another 13 armoured cars to put them back to service.

One of the greatest achievements of the 39 M. Csaba armoured cars connected to the battle around Uman in late July early August 1941, where the Hungarian Mobile Corps played a vital role to prevent the escape of the Soviet troops out of the encirclement.

The 1st Cavalry Brigade took part in the successful operations against the Uman pocket. On 6 August, the commander of the brigade, Major General Antal Vattay, ordered the armoured cavalry battalion to reconnoitre the area around Golovanevsk, where the encircled Red Army units were located. The reconnaissance force consisted of one bicycle platoon and an armoured car platoon with three 39 M. Csaba armoured cars and was led by Ensign László Merész. The Ensign led two Csabas on the road to Moldovka, keeping the third in reserve with the bicycle platoon.The two advancing 39 M. Csaba armoured cars surprised two Cossack cavalry squadrons on the road, the 39 M. Csaba armoured cars opened fire from point-blank range and annihilated the soviet cavalry troops. Later on, Soviet motorised troops of 20 trucks and around 200 riflemen approached the killing fields on the road, trying to break through the encirclement. The Csabas opened fire again with their anti-tank rifles and machine guns. During the contact, the armoured cars exhausting their ammunition, firing 12,000 machine-gun bullets and 720 20mm shells. The Hungarian armoured cars succeeded in halting the Soviet troops of the 6th Army and sealed the gap in the encirclement. For his actions during this operation, Ensign Merész was decorated with the Great Gold Officer Bravery Medal.

1st Reconnaissance Battalion on the Eastern Front 1942/43

The 1st Reconnaissance Battalion was led by Lieutenant Colonel István Vaska, his unit belonged to the 1st Armoured Field Division. The 1st Reconnaissance Battalion took part in the summer bridgehead battles at the River Don in 1942. By that time the terrain and the determined enemy resistance did not favour the deployment of the armoured cars. Their weapons were too light and their armour protection too weak even against the Soviet anti-tank rifles. The technical losses of the 1st Armoured Field Division were 10 39 M. Csaba armoured cars during the campaign 1942-1943.

Armoured Car Troops with the Occupation Forces in Ukraine, 1941-44

The 102nd Independent Armoured was organised by the 1/II Tank Battalion in 1943. The Company had two light tank platoons with three-three 38 M. Toldi light tanks and two armoured car platoons with three-three 39 M. Csaba armoured cars. The Company was commanded by Major Zoltán Parázsó. The task of the Company was to provide a mobile reserve for the Occupation Force East. The unit was deployed in December 1943 to Kremenyec, later moved to Stanislau.

Ensign Arthur Russ carried out reconnaissance at Flusto Miasto with his 39 M. Csaba armoured on 23 March 1944, when he was ambushed by Soviet tanks, he wounded and left behind, reported missing, probably killed in action. Posthumously he was decorated with the Hungarian Knight Cross with swords. However, he was captured by the Soviet forces; he was in the prison of war, survived it and just returned to Hungary in 1948.

In 1943 the VII Bicycle Battalion was also deployed within the Occupation Forces, with two bicycle companies, and one armoured car and one support company. The armoured car company had 8 x 39 M. Csaba armoured cars.

The 2nd Armoured Division in Galicia, 1944

The division was equipped totally with Hungarian produced armoured vehicles, among them were 14 x 39 M. and 40 M. Csaba armoured cars. The 2nd Reconnaissance Battalion was deployed from Kassa (Kosice) led by Lieutenant Colonel László Wolf.

On 13 April, the 2nd Reconnaissance battalion occupied the Lukwa passage and Rosulna and clashed with the Soviet rear guards west of Nadworna. The Hungarians lost one killed and three wounded and two 39 M. Csaba armoured cars, one 38 M. Botond truck and one car were destroyed.

By the early dawn of 17 April, the Hungarian troops have occupied their starting positions. The Sándor Group consisted of the 3/II Tank Battalion, 4th Motorised Rifle, 2nd Reconnaissance and 2nd Light Artillery Battalions. The 2nd Reconnaissance Battalion and the 3rd Motorized Sapper Company arrived in Solotwina. About 20.00 hours the 2nd Reconnaissance Battalion reached the Bystrica-Nadwornianska River west of Nadworna, but it was not possible to cross the bridge on this site. During this clash, two 39 M. Csaba armoured cars and one 38 M. Botond truck was lost there.

On 18 April the Sándor group launched its new attack at dawn, but the bridge to the west of the city was destroyed. The Hungarian sappers repaired the bridge under the enemy fire, and the troops of the 2nd Reconnaissance Battalion broke into Nadworna around 10.00 hours. They were supported by artillery fire. Then, in strenuous street fighting, the stubbornly resisting Soviet rear guards were eliminated at 19.00 hours. Until 12 May only two 39 M. Csaba armoured car was lost because the Hungarian deployed cautiously their armoured vehicles.

During the Soviet offensive, the reconnaissance troops were deployed again to slow down the enemy advance. On 26 July the 2nd Reconnaissance Battalion broke out of the Soviet encirclement at Klaus and reached Nowicza.

According to the combat report of the 2nd Armoured Division, the majority of their vehicles were lost or needed significant repair. The 2nd Reconnaissance Battalion were lucky to lose only two to three 39 M. Csaba armoured cars during the operations.

The 1st Cavalry Division in Russia

The 3rd Reconnaissance Battalion belonged to the 1st Cavalry Division with two armoured car companies numbering 27 Csaba armoured cars. According some sources the battalion was deployed with only one armoured car company equipped with 13 Csaba armoured cars.

The 39 M. Csaba armoured cars were painted in three-tone camouflage in the summer of 1940, this car belonged to the 1st Reconnaissance Battalion wearing the white lightning bolt and Maltese cross military insignia. The number plate Pc.123 is painted into a white square. (Szollár János)

The 1st Reconnaissance Battalion had the octagonal military insignia in the summer of 1941. The platoon sign, the white heart was painted inside the left upper corner of the military insignia. (Mujzer collection)

39 M. Csaba armoured car belonged to the 2nd Reconnaissance Battalion, the original camouflage was over sprayed with a winter camouflage. The white triangle was the divisional sign of the 2nd Armoured Division; the white German-style eagle was the battalion sign. (Fortepan)

Lieutenant Colonel József Bányai led the 3rd Reconnaissance Battalion, where Captain Rolan Koós was the company commander of the 1st Armoured Car Company. After the deployment of the Cavalry Division, the 3rd Reconnaissance Battalion had only 6 armoured cars remaining from its original 23.

The 2nd Armoured Division in Transylvania 1944

Due to the losses suffered in Galicia, the combat strength of the division was depleted. According to the reports it still had 12 x 39 M. and 40 M. Csaba armoured cars. The 2nd Reconnaissance Battalion took part in the offensive against the Romanian forces on 07 September 1944. During that day one of the 39 M. Csaba armoured cars of the battalion was lost at Mezőszengyel. Reserve Ensign László Burka's armoured car came under an artillery barrage and fallen into a ravine and the ensign died of his head wounds.

In the early days of December 1944, the Division still had 8 x 39 M. Csaba armoured cars. By the end of this month, 100 armoured vehicles were written off from the battle order of the 2nd Armoured Division, among them were Csaba armoured cars too.

1st Armoured Division in 1944/45

The 1st Reconnaissance Battalion was commanded by Lieutenant Colonel Imre Németh. The battalion had one-one armour, motorcycle and motorised rifle companies. The battalion was lack of the armoured car company and fire and combat support platoons. It had a composite armoured company where the 39 M. Csaba armoured cars and 38 M. Toldi light tanks of the Division were assembled.

The 1st Reconnaissance Battalion which was part of the second wave of the attack chased the withdrawing Romanian troops and occupied Arad. At 07.15 p.m. on September 13, the Hungarian troops occupied the town and its bridges intact. Only the 1st Reconnaissance Battalion was ordered to continue the attack, and it arrived on the west side of the Maros Valley on 14 September. The withdrawing Romanian forces built up a defence line at the area of Paulis, along the River Maros (Mures), behind a tank ditch.

Siege of Budapest 1944-1945

The Hungarian Police and the Gendarme units also had armoured subunits with antiquated 35 M. FIAT Ansaldo tankettes and 39 M. Csaba armoured cars encircled in Budapest. The Galánta Gendarmerie Battalion, totalling 500 men led by Major István Szili, had one-one light tank company had 10-10 35 M. FIAT Ansaldo and 38 M. Toldi tanks, and 39 M. Csaba armoured cars. The Gendarmerie Armoured Company stationed at Hüvösvölgy at the barracks of the Bólyai Military Academy.

The police forces were also involved in the defence of the city. The Police Assault Battalion launched a counter-attack against advancing Russian troops at Vecsés, Andrássy-telep on 01 November 1944. The police were supported by five 39 M. Csaba armoured cars, the police troops wore dark blue uniforms and Adrian helmets which surprised the Soviet troops. The Soviets easily knocked out three 39 M. Csaba armoured cars during the battle.

The remaining 39 M. and 40 M. Csaba armoured cars were lost during the fighting in Hungary between 1944 and 1945. The left-behind knocked out or abandoned vehicles were collected as scrap metal for recycling.

40 M. Csaba command/signal armoured car belonged to the 1st Armoured Pioneer Battalion in 1944, the battalion sign, half-circle was painted into the white rhombus divisional sign next to the small scale military insignia. (Deák Tamás)

The Ludovika Military Academy also got 39 M. Csaba armoured cars, during the summer exercises the armoured cars got a white L45 tactical number painted on the turret. (Mujzer collection)

CAMOUFLAGE AND MARKINGS

The Hungarian armoured vehicles manufactured from 1940 were finished in French-style camouflage consisting of a base colour of dark olive green with light ochre and red-brown blotches. Until 1942, this disruptive camouflage was brush-applied with hard-edged patterns of irregular blotches. However, in 1942 the Hungarians began to use spray equipment, giving the camouflage patterns a more diaphanous appearance.

During the deployment of the 1st Armoured Field Division in 1942, the Hungarian made armoured vehicles; Toldi light tanks, Nimród self-propelled autocannons and Csaba armoured cars were repainted to "panzer" grey, similar to the Pz.IVF-1 and Skoda 38(t) tanks.

In 1944, some of the armoured and non-armoured vehicles were uniformly painted dark green. In April 1944, at least one Csaba armoured car platoon of the 2nd Reconnaissance Battalion was overpainted in German-style light ochre. In 1944, two to five 39 M. Csaba armoured cars were handed over to the mobile reserve of the State Police. The known two Csabas, RR-711 and -712 were painted dark bright blue.

The vehicles of the 1st Reconnaissance Battalion deployed to the River Don, got whitewashed camouflage during the winter of 1942-1943. The Krupp Protze large command car, the 40 M. Csaba command/signal armoured car and the side-car motor-bicycle belonged to the battalion staff. (Markó Ferenc)

National Military Insignia

In 1940, temporary military insignias were developed by the battalions and the higher echelons. The 1st Reconnaissance Battalion used a white Maltese cross as a base in 1940. The green or red outlines and the circle were to be painted in different combinations for each company of the battalion. The insignia was painted on all four sides and, for aerial identification, onto the engine deck too. The Csaba armoured cars had the insignia painted onto the turret sides too. The vehicles of the 2nd Reconnaissance Battalion had a green cross outlined in white over a red circular base painted on five places, was allowed to use it up to the end of 1941.

Finally, Mobile Corps Command and the Institute of Military Technology jointly developed the octagonal insignia consisting of a green cross outlined in white and the area between the arms of the cross filled with red in 1941. It became the standard military insignia from 1941 until 1942. The insignia should be painted onto the sides, front, rear and the top (engine deck) of vehicles. The insignia in practice resulted to be too large and colourful. The insignia on the front hull, behind where sat the driver on Csaba armoured cars made a perfect aiming-point for enemy anti-tank gunners. Therefore in the field crews often covered the front insignia with mud.

In November 1942 a new, insignia came into service, already used by the air force - white cross over a black square - authorised in three different sizes according to the location on the vehicles. The instructions required the insignia to be placed on all visible sides of vehicles, but in practice, it was applied only to the sides and in increased size to the engine deck.

Unit Insignias

From 1938, each unit invented its own colourful unit identification signs. Later, the standard requirements were to use adaptations of easy geometrical symbols. As of 1942 the units started to use the basic geometrical symbols, painted on the front and back mud-guards or the hull. The Armoured Corps regulated the unit signs of the subordinated units in 1943. In 1944, the division and regiment (battalion) signs were painted on the left and right front and rear hull or mud-guards. The non-armoured vehicles also carried unit signs, following the above-mentioned regulations.

License Plates

The armoured vehicles had painted licence plates. On the armoured cars, the front serial number was shown in a thin white rectangle. The style was usually a Pc. (abbreviation of the armoured car) with the national shield (red-white-green), followed by a three-digit serial number. The letters and the numbers were painted in black. The same serial numbers were on the rear of the hull but in a square shape. Later, from 1944, the front license plate was simply painted on the camouflage without white background.

Tactical Numbering

Hungarian armoured vehicles adopted the use of three-four digits turret numbers in 1942. The 2nd Reconnaissance Battalion used three-digit tactical numbers on the Csaba armoured cars, painted on the rear plate of the turret. The Ludovica Military Academy used big L and two digits tactical numbers on summer exercises.

The Pc.158 Csaba armoured car got a sand yellow camouflage, and had a three-digit tactical number, 133 painted on the back of the turret. (ECPA)

BIBLIOGRAPHY

Bíró Ádám – Éder Miklós – Sárhidai Gyula: A magyar királyi honvédség külföldi gyártású páncélos harcjárművei 1920-1945, Petit Real, 2006

Bíró Ádám – Éder Miklós – Sárhidai Gyula: A magyar királyi honvédség hazai gyártású páncélos harcjárművei 1920- 1945, Petit Real, 2012

Bonhardt Attila – Sárhidai Gyula – Winkler Róbert: A magyar királyi honvédség fegyverzete 1919-45 part 1, Zrínyi, 1992

Dombrády Loránd: A magyar gazdaság és a hadfelszerelés, 1938/44, Akadémia, 1981

Csima János: Források a Magyar Honvédség II. világháborús történetének tanulmányozásához, Zrínyi, 1961

Hajdú Ferenc – Sárhidai Gyula: A magyar királyi honvéd Haditechnikai Intézettől a HM Technológiai Hivatalig, HM Technológiai Hivatal 2005

Horváth Csaba: A magyar katonai felderítés története a kezdetektől 1945-ig, Puedlo

Horváth Csaba – Lengyel Ferenc: A délvidéki hadművelet 1940, Puedlo

Illésfalvi Péter – Szabó Péter – Számvéber Norbert: Erdély a Hadak Útján 1940-1944, Puedlo

Illésfalvi Péter – Kovács Vilmos – Maruzs Roland: Vitézségért, HK Hermanos, 2011

Mujzer Péter: PÁNCÉLOSOK, a magyar páncélos fegyvernem és a rohamtüzérség története 1938-1945, Magánkiadás Budapest 2019.

Szabó Péter – Számvéber Norbert: A keleti hadszíntér és Magyarország 1941- 1943, Puedlo

Szabó Péter – Számvéber Norbert: Magyarország és a keleti hadszíntér 1943-1945, Puedlo

Ungváry Krisztián: A magyar honvédség a második világháborúban, Osiris, 2005

Dr. vitéz Tóth József: A volt m. kir. 1. honvéd felderítő zászlóalj története, Magánkiadás, Budapest 2006.

ARTICLES

Hadtörténeti Közlemények:

Tóth Lajos: A Gyorshadtest a Szovjetunióban, HK 1966/2
Dombrándy Loránd: A horthysta katonai vezetés erőfeszítései a páncélos fegyvernem megteremtésére, HK 1969/2, 1970/4
Illésfalvi Péter: A hegyicsapatok megszervezése a Magyar királyi Honvédségnél 1939-1940-ben, HK 2000/4
Simon Gábor: A német XI. hadtest részvétele a magyar 1. hadsereg hadműveletében HK 126. 2013/4

Haditechnikai Szemle:

Bíró Ádám: The AC-II, 39 M. Csaba páncélgépkocsik, 1992/3
Dr. Mujzer Péter: A magyar páncélos fegyvernem szervezeti és fegyverzeti fejlesztése 1938-1942 I. rész, 2016/2
Dr. Mujzer Péter: A magyar páncélos fegyvernem szervezeti és fegyverzeti fejlesztése 1938-1942 II. rész, 2016/3
Dr. Mujzer Péter: A Magyar Királyi honvédség páncélos csapatainak végső szervezete 1942-1944, 2016/4
Dr. Mujzer Péter: A Magyar Királyi Honvédség páncélos csapatainak képzési rendszere, 2016/5
Dr. Mujzer Péter: Magyar páncélosok alkalmazása a II. világháborúban II. rész, 2017/1
Dr. Mujzer Péter:A Magyar Királyi Honvédség páncélos szervezeteinek részvétele a Szovjetunió elleni hadműveletekben 1941-ben, 2017/3
Dr. Mujzer Péter: Magyar páncélos csapatok a keleti fronton 1942-43, I. rész, 2017/4
Dr. Mujzer Péter: Magyar páncélos csapatok a keleti fronton 1942-43 II. rész, 2017/5
Dr. Mujzer Péter: A 2. páncéloshadosztály hadműveletei Galiciában 1944-ben, I. rész, 2017/6
Dr. Mujzer Péter: A 2. páncéloshadosztály hadműveletei Galiciában 1944-ben, II. rész, 2018/1
Dr. Mujzer Péter: A magyar megszálló erők páncélos alakulatai, 2018/2
Somkutas Róbert: A Magyar Királyi Honvédség páncélozott eszközökkel felszerelt felderítő csapatai I. rész, 2016/1
Somkutas Róbert: A Magyar Királyi Honvédség páncélozott eszközökkel felszerelt felderítő csapatai II. rész, 2016/2
Somkutas Róbert: A Magyar Királyi Honvédség páncélozott eszközökkel felszerelt felderítő csapatai III. rész, 2016/3
Somkutas Róbert: A Magyar Királyi Honvédség páncélozott eszközökkel felszerelt felderítő csapatai IV. rész, 2016/4
Somkutas Róbert: A Magyar Királyi Honvédség páncélozott eszközökkel felszerelt felderítő csapatai V. rész, 2016/5
Somkutas Róbert: A Magyar Királyi Honvédség páncélozott eszközökkel felszerelt felderítő csapatai VI. rész, 2016/6
Somkutas Róbert: A Magyar Királyi Honvédség páncélozott eszközökkel felszerelt felderítő csapatai VII. rész, 2017/2
Somkutas Róbert: A Magyar Királyi Honvédség páncélozott eszközökkel felszerelt felderítő csapatai VIII. rész, 2017/3
Somkutas Róbert: A Magyar Királyi Honvédség páncélozott eszközökkel felszerelt felderítő csapatai IX. rész, 2017/4
Somkutas Róbert: A Magyar Királyi Honvédség páncélozott eszközökkel felszerelt felderítő csapatai X. rész, 2017/5
Somkutas Róbert: A Magyar Királyi Honvédség páncélozott eszközökkel felszerelt felderítő csapatai XI. rész, 2017/6

Belvedere

GALLó Krisztián: Páncélosok a Kárpátokban, 2003/XV. 1-2, 3-4., 5-6.

Militaria Modell:

Éder Miklós: Magyar páncélos járművek alakulat jelzései, 1. rész, 1991 / 1
Éder Miklós: Magyar páncélos járművek alakulat jelzései, 2. rész, 1991/2
Éder Miklós: 39 M. Csaba páncélgépkocsi, 1992/1
Éder Miklós: Magyar páncélosok hadi jelzése, 1917-1945, 1992/6

Pro Modell

Mujzer Péter: A magyar királyi honvédség páncélos csapatainak jelzésrendszere, 2003/1-3

Foreign Books

Dr Tamás Baczoni – Dr László Tóth: Hungarian Army Uniforms 1939 – 1945, HUNIFORM 2010
Csaba Becze: Magyar steel, Mashroom Publication, 2006
Dénes Bernád, Charles K. Kliment: Magyar Warriors, The history of the Royal Hungarian Armed Forces 1919-1945, volume 1, Helion Publication, 2015
Dénes Bernád, Charles K. Kliment: Magyar Warriors, The history of the Royal Hungarian Armed Forces 1919-1945, volume 2, Helion Publication, 2017
Patrick Cloutier: Three Kings: Axis Royal Armies on the Russian Front 1941, 2014
Military Intelligence Division: Order of Battle and Handbook of the Hungarian Armed Forces, 1944 US War Dep. (restricted)
Péter Mujzer: Hungarian Mobile Forces 1920-45, Bayside Books, 2000
Péter Mujzer: Huns on Wheels, Hungarian Mobile Forces in WWII, Armoured, Cavalry, Bicycle Troops, Motorised Rifle, Mujzer and Partners Ltd., 2015
Péter Mujzer: Hungarian Armoured Forces in WWII, KAGERO Books, PHOTOSNIPER 26., Lublin 2017
Péter Mujzer: Operational History of the Hungarian Armoured Troops in WW2, KAGERO, Photosniper 28., Lublin 2018.

Péter Mujzer: Hungarian Soldier versus Soviet Soldier, Eastern Front 1941, Osprey Publishing, Oxford 2021.

Péter Mujzer: Hungarian Arms and Armours of World War Two, KEY Publishing, Stamford 2021.

Péter Mujzer: Barbarossa Campaign in 1941 Hungarian perspective, KAGERO, Lublin 2021.

Leo Niehorster: The Royal Hungarian Army 1920-45, Bayside Books, 1998
Nigel Thomas- László Pál Szabó: The Royal Hungarian Army in World War II, Ospery, 2008
Anthony Tucker-Jones: Armored warfare and Hitler's allies 1941-1945, Pen&Sword, 2013
Steven Zaloga- James Grandsen: The Eastern Front, Arms and Armour, 1983
Steven Zaloga: Tanks of Hitler's Eastern allies 1941-45, Osprey, 2013